SCATTERED THOUGHTS, MEMOIRS, AND DREAMS OF A STILETTO QUEEN

BY SYBIL THEBAUD-BRIERRE

DEDICATION

I want to dedicate this book to three people.

Firstly, to my daughter Cassandra Marie for always encouraging me to write and get my story out there to the world. Besides being my biggest supporter all along, she also provided much-needed feedback.

Secondly, to my beloved mother who went through so much particularly during the last years of her life. She always believed that someday she would prevail and tell her story. Since she is no longer here, I am her voice and vessel.

And lastly, to my Sista friend, Martine, who recently passed unexpectedly at the young age of 44. It is because of her I realized that tomorrow is not promised to love, laugh, and live.

I would also like to add a special thanks to Monsieur Pierre Lespinasse who helped me get started on this literary journey.

Table of Contents

INTRODUCTION

While growing up, one of my favorite movies was *Gigi*. I loved watching this musical with my mother who, of course, loved it as well, particularly due to it being set in "Gay Par-EE." Bougie Haitians love anything that has to do with the French. The movie is about a young girl in a family of courtesans. She is being groomed to be one as well. An old family friend and rich playboy, Gaston, makes an offer to her grandmother and grand aunt to take her as his mistress; offering everything money can buy, but also offering a life of infamy. She knows she will become a well-known courtesan and her future will revolve around going from one rich man to another; something Gigi doesn't want. After much back and forth at the end of the movie Gigi finally got what she wanted and married Gaston.

My mother always said that she was like Gigi. She always knew what she wanted in life, and that she wasn't ready to be a second choice, rather the first. My mother had an ex-boyfriend who dumped her for a woman who could advance his political ambition while offering her the option of becoming the second best. But that wasn't enough for my mother who held onto her goal and desire and got the marriage proposal she required. Due to this fact, my mother would always say that I was someone who didn't know what I wanted in life, and she was absolutely right about that. I didn't know what I wanted, and that's the reason I was so easily manipulated into following my boyfriend/child's father's dreams and goals. He was a rapper back in the early 90s, and I was satisfied with being his girl. I started playing the wifey[1] role once I followed him into a life in an "Islamic" cult, giving up my family, friends, my home, and dignity. Fortunately, because I purposely became a mother at the tender age of 21, I got out and had no choice but to figure out what I wanted and had to do in life.

Since I came from a Cosbyish background with my father as a physician, I naturally returned to college after years of being told that it was the

---

[1] wifey-pretend wife; not legally a wife

only way to guarantee overall success in life. Mulling over the thought of being a single mother, I had to break the cycle and shame of no formal education. After I graduated and got married, I tried to fall into the line of getting a job like everyone else. But finding employment proved a daunting task to achieve. Most of the job offers I got were more of the same. Telemarketing, data entry, etc. low level and low-paying jobs not even requiring that you have a college degree. Even though the goal was to be able to take care of my daughter and I, I knew I wanted a job that was in line with my degree in psychology. I knew I wanted to use my experience to help young women, particularly teenagers to avoid what I had been through in life. But I recall at one point while I was mingling at my neighbor's party, I was told that it was best to focus on financial ambitions even though my goal was altruistic. Well, finding steady work that paid well proved nearly impossible especially after getting my master's. The awful experience of having a master's degree and trying to find suitable employment made me realize that education is no longer the key to a better life. This experience led me to write this book which started with voicing out my complaints and anger about my career/financial life, but also got me to open up and reveal my unruly teen years, questionable 20s, tricky 30s, and challenging 40s.

Through writing, I started to realize that there are probably a lot of young girls out there who are like me; no clue of where their life is going, or what they want to do. Without direction, it's easy to get sucked into someone else's dreams/goals. After my personal experience, the consecutive loss of my parents, plus, the untimely death of my friends, I've become too aware that life is so fragile. None of us are guaranteed our time here. We need to fulfill our purposes while we're still here. So, for those young girls who are wandering aimlessly, I want to guide you to discover your true potential. Also, besides focusing on conventional careers that require a college degree, I want to emphasize careers that don't require a college education. I know that even though I succeeded academically, I wasn't meant to go to regular colleges. I loved sketching and designing women's clothes. I wanted to be a fashion designer, but it wasn't something that was encouraged in my household. Only conservative degree occupations were allowed. Many young people probably want to explore careers in the arts such as dance, music, acting, and art itself. Or what about those who like cooking and baking, or those who like fixing things, building things, and making gadgets work right. I want to provide a platform that focuses on helping young women discover their likes and use that to find what they can do in life. Plus, not everyone is meant for a college education, and not too many places would stress in exploring the alternative, and therefore, I would like to offer areas that emphasize that. In addition to my career experiences, I would like to also add my two cents to something I feel goes hand in hand particularly when it comes to us girls – self-esteem and dealing with men. Now, am I an expert? Absolutely not, but after some 40 plus years on this earth, I have learned a couple of things. One being as we age, we change our way of thinking. The way I thought as a teenager/young adult is zero quality compared to the way I think now. Now sometimes with age does come wisdom and I've decided to pass along what I now know. So, even though I'm not famous, haven't been on a reality show riding on my fame, haven't cured a life-threatening disease or found the missing link, I am however a daughter, mother, wife, and grandmother who has more or less learned some life lessons that I want to share as well as fulfill one of my goals by helping others find their purpose in life.

So, as you take a glimpse into my life, at the tip of your fingers, know that I've made a series of mistakes and have had some bad things happen to me. Through these experiences, I realized my path was being shaped. So, instead of letting them keep me back, I've decided to move toward better things in my life. Like my beloved mother before me, I now know that I'm meant for better and greater things. Thank you for allowing me to share my life experiences with you.

OVEREDUCATED & UNDEREMPLOYED

When I graduated from college, my cousins got me a briefcase as a gift. My mother said it was their way of saying 'go back to school and get your master's/doctorate'. Haitian families deadass[2] believe that the more educated you are, the more successful in life you will be. Growing up I was always told that 'if you get a college degree your life would automatically be successful, you would never know struggle, and all doors would open up for you'.

As a C+ and occasional B- student my parents had their work cut out for them. I wasn't really interested in school and had to endure the nightly ritual of doing homework with my father, who would get very angry at me if I didn't provide the correct answer to questions asked. Thanks to a belt lashing, I'll never forget what six times four is. My parents, though loving, tended to hold their affection back and vehemently show their disapproval of my academic failures. I'll never forget one summer when school was ending my mother came for the awards ceremony with her friend, a classmate's mother. Her friend's children got several awards while I got none. When my father came to pick us up, I was so happy and excited to see him as he was with me, but all that changed the moment my mother and I got in the car. She proceeded to show him my report card and told him how I embarrassed her because I didn't get any awards. My father just looked at my report card and talked about how I went down in vital subjects, and how I'd never be able to go to college with such grades. His once happy smile turned to a permanent scowl on our drive home. It was then I realized that not doing well in school was a way of losing my parents' love, and something that would also affect my future.

As I got older, I stayed as an average student doing good enough to get by, but never honor student material. During my senior year in high school, I decided that I wanted to be a TV anchorwoman, so I enrolled in the New York Institute of Technology and majored in

---

[2] deadass-seriously

Communications Arts. My father's best friend and my godfather, also a physician, told me that "I was going to a Mickey Mouse college" and how disappointed he was in me while stating that I was ruining my life. Well, imagine everyone's faces when I decided to drop out of college and follow my boyfriend into a life of submission and servitude in Islam. Severe disappointment turned into severe outrage when I eventually came back home with my clothes in a trash bag, and the extra baggage of a 20 weeks pregnancy, to be exact. I had automatically turned into a statistic of a single, Black, unwed and improperly educated mother. My life was over without a formal education;how was I to support this impending child? I was an instant candidate for welfare and as a first generation daughter of upwardly mobile Haitian parents that was totally out of the question. In order to break the cycle of shame and consistency in Black America, my parents insisted that I enroll in college after the birth of my daughter. Another part of my condition was that I had to get a part-time job and would heavily rely on financial aid and loans. My father paid for my school bills from the onset, but I lollygagged and wasted my time and his money. I got a temporary job that eventually became permanent at a local retail bank in a CALL CENTER. Now some must be asking why I capitalized these words in bold form. Well, these two words would follow and haunt me down for the remainder of my job/career hunting. I didn't do so well during my first year back in school, so I ended up dropping out of two classes and failing one. Pops was furious and told my mother that if I didn't buckle down and take this seriously, I would have to leave the house.

The following semester I did a little bit better with two B's, a D, and an F in math. I enrolled in summer school for a while and tried for about three weeks before finally dropping out. Working part-time, taking care of a small child, and trying to balance some sense of a social life to keep me sane; school wasn't really on my list of priorities. My mother couldn't help but keep telling me countless times how all the kids I grew up with, and who were younger than me were now all ahead of me. Hurry up and get your degree she kept telling me again and again. One day she was watching *The Maury Povich Show* when they were interviewing girls who had become strippers to pay their way through college. She made a comment saying that some people would go to any length to get educated and have a degree, while others like myself don't even care.

Around my second year, I started to focus on making a significant improvement in my life. At the time, I was involved in a serious relationship with my future husband and I was eager to start my life all over again. I went from a C- minus student to a strong B+. I got my Associates in December 1995 from SUNY Farmingdale and transferred to SUNY Stony Brook in January 1996 in order to continue my stride of semi-excellence. With pressure from my family and now myself, I decided to take summer courses in order to graduate earlier than the full two years. By May 1997 I graduated with a Bachelor of Arts in Psychology and a minor in Africana Studies. My father was so ecstatically happy that he couldn't help but cry. This truly was the best moment of my life, I was in seventh heaven. I finally made up for the disgrace that I brought on to my family and made everything right once again. I recall my godfather making the champagne toast by saying, "Thank you Sybile for finally making us proud."

So after a much-needed summer vacay in September of 1997, I was armed and ready to find a job, but no one told me it would be so hard. Everyone kept telling me to be patient that it takes time, but little did I know that it would be three years before I could find my first real employment. Back then all I wanted was a job that could make me $400 a week including benefits, so I could make my way as a working woman and be able to take care of my daughter and myself. Tired of being constantly rejected, I made my way to an employment agency. I'll never forget the words of the lady at the agency when she told me, "You're never gonna get $10 an hour so you need to ask for $8 an hour." Resigned and full of resolution I accepted that insult, but regardless, not much came my way in permanent jobs. There were temporary jobs here and there until I finally took matters into my own hands and took a permanent job at my home turf, a CALL CENTER. First, I started working at the DIME now Chase, and then CMS Works. I hated both jobs because a college degree wasn't required, and I worked with people who I felt were below my level. I mean I was fed this bullcrap from the cradle, and it wasn't going to change anytime soon. Additionally, working in the real world you will have to deal with a level of disrespect and disdain that is more than mind-blowing. These jobs (in my opinion most jobs in general) cripple employees to suffer indignation because they think they have no other alternatives.

Finally in 2000, married with two kids, I got my first job requiring a college degree. It was for an HR outsourcing firm working in training and development. This was the first job I ever had that paid me a salary, offered me benefits and insurance; I felt like I had finally made it. During the first week of my employment, the boss surprisingly gave everyone a $1500 raise. I felt like I had hit the lottery. I really enjoyed working there during my first year. It was quite flexible with hours plus overtime, and stipends were handed left and right. Plus, they fed us lunch and sometimes breakfast daily. Things were good for a while, but then the economy changed. The company lost most of its clientele and work became scarce. I maintained my position, but I grew tired and frustrated with the repetitiveness. I wanted to be challenged and considering the fact that the cost of living and my expenses were going up. I then realized that I would need to focus on beginning a career and not just obtaining a job. So, after speaking with a co-worker who completed her Masters in Human Resource Management I decided to go that route as well. I returned to Stony Brook University and enrolled in the fall of 2002. Determined and focused, I planned out my career. The program normally took two years to conclude, so I decided to go from full-time to part-time at work and focus on getting my degree in one year. My supervisor let me know that by going part-time I would not only intentionally cut my hours, but since our work was based on supply and demand, I would be available only when needed. The future looked so bright that this was seen as a minor bump on the road to achieving my dream. Isn't that what people have always said, "You have to make sacrifices in order to be successful." So, I made the supreme decision to sacrifice a huge part of my finances thinking it would come back to me tenfold. For the first time in my life, I had a goal and a clear direction for myself, my life, and the lives of my children. Well, after losing sleep in order to study for many exams, writing papers, and giving several presentations, I graduated in December 2003 with an average of 3.7. My father again cried tears of joy. Not only did his little girl who dropped out years ago had acquired a bachelors, but masters as well. I remember after all the festivities were done and over, I asked my mother if she thinks I would have the same problems I had before getting started on my career. She replied, "Oh no, I don't think so." Those words haunt me to this day.

Laws of attraction gurus would simply say that the reason my search ended in such dismay is that I put it out there. With all due respect to positive thinkers... that's some bullshit. A singular mention of this could not fully impact my life for the next 10 years. I mean I "did" everything right. I worked for an HR firm, joined the national organization for HR, and paid $200 a year that I didn't have, plus I had additional education. At first, I thought it was only natural to get no callbacks or responses, but then it started getting frustrating especially when I applied for a $75,000.00 a year job in the city, and the hiring manager asked what I could bring to the table. I proudly answered 'my masters'. He proceeded to tear me a new one[3] . It was so indoctrinated in me regarding education that naturally, that was my response. Fed up but not down, I continued to go through the career websites and kept sending my resumes to various organizations. At one point I even got dressed up and went to Roosevelt Field Mall and handed my resume to Bloomingdale's, Nordstrom, and Macy's. It struck me as funny when I remembered it was the same mall that I and my friend, Anna, decided one Friday night to dress up and go find guys that I was now dressing up to find a job. I was unable to go back full-time at my job due to the demand and the fact that my supervisor and I never got along. I don't do well when it comes to office politics cheesin and kissing ass. Also, my boss at the time was an undercover racist bitch who is probably voting for Trump as I write this now. (GOD help us with this election) So, I decided to

---

[3] tear me a new one-scold or criticize someone harshly

take a huge leap of faith and walk away after five years with no safety net. Everyone said it was a mistake to walk away without a job assurance elsewhere, but I had faith and my "treasured education." I finally found a job two months later as a temp associate for an electronics company in their HR department making $15 an hour. For me, it was like finding a needle in the haystack. My co-workers, who were whites, complained I shouldn't settle but for me, I felt this was a stepping stone necessary to get to the top. After three months, I was offered an interview for a permanent position. I was interviewed on Friday afternoon for the position, and I was told my responsibility would increase in the HR department. I truly felt things were starting to go my way until Monday morning, I received a call from the employment agency informing me my assignment was over. Perplexed and confused, I couldn't understand what had happened. A week ago everything was fine, and after my interview, I was led to believe that the position was mine. Then in one instance, it was gone.

Turns out that this was just the beginning of a miserable existence for me, and despite much effort on my part I remained unemployed for over a year. I started to feel as if something or someone was out to get me . Or like it had something to do with me especially after a particular job interview. I went to my scheduled appointment on time and sat around and waited for the hiring manager for about a good 30-40 minutes, but he never showed up. I spoke to the only other person there and he sheepishly apologized and told me to come back the following week. Since I had no other opportunities I went back and the same shit happened again. This time after approaching the same guy, I got angry and walked out. One time via email, I received an offer to interview for an HR job paying $90,000 annually. I was flabbergasted and replied instantly to set up an interview. As I researched the company I found no legit information, and I never heard from anyone regarding my response. Again, I received another email regarding an HR job paying $85,000 from the same people. This time I sent a reply email raining curses on them. This situation might have been a little bit more bearable if my husband was employed, but when it rains it pours and he ended up losing the job he had for 15 years without any employment compensation. With no income whatsoever we had to apply for Medicaid. I never thought that as someone with a master's degree I would end up on line at social services, but I did. So much for graduating from a credible university instead of a "Mickey Mouse" college huh.

I was disillusioned, disappointed, and more than anything angry. I worked my ass off and did the right thing, so how the hell did I end up in poverty. I was supposed to be making $55,000 to start as an HR associate/coordinator, saving money, and being able to buy all the nice things I wanted and dreamed of for myself and my kids. I was also trying to be independent and self-sufficient from my parents and wanted to work on getting a home of my own. This wasn't supposed to be like this. One time I overheard my father complaining to my mother about my husband saying he wasn't able to provide for his family, but my mother interjected by stating I'm a three time college graduate and I should be able to support my family by myself. Speaking of my parents, can you imagine how they felt after feeding me this bullshit of being educated and never struggling to see me in this perpetual state of unemployment? I recall telling them that what they taught me to believe was wrong, and you know what their response was……. 'I STUDIED THE WRONG THING'. I should have studied nursing.. Everybody knows that besides rice Haitians love nursing. Being a nurse is like being Moses, and the Red Sea parts for you. Since pops had the inside scoop he knew that nurses with overtime made as much as he did, and were always in demand. I disliked anything medical/scientific and I wasn't about to go back to school again.

After applying for every job under the sun, even willing to go as far as the city which is a lot for someone with a pigeon phobia, having worked temporarily in a department store as a seasonal recruiter making $10.00 an hour, I finally found employment as a bill collector at an oil company's CALL CENTER making $14 an hour. Besides the holiday recruiter position, this was my lowest point. I worked with people who mostly had high school diplomas, and at one point I was trained by someone who was a high school dropout. Although I made it and stayed

10

for three years, it was not without some uproar. Since this job was on the lowest level on the totem pole there was no such thing as a grace period when you are late. If you were one minute late it was held against you. One day I was eight minutes late coming back from lunch and I was docked that time from my pay. The job I currently hold now, I was once 10 minutes late coming back from lunch. Not only did I get my regular pay, but no one ever said anything to me. Even though I hated that job with such a passion I ended up being the unofficial trainer and contributed to their much-needed training manual. Because of my work and work ethic, I was offered a team leader position but was told that I needed to work full time six days straight for eight hours a day. Though I definitely would have welcomed the extra income and status upgrade, I did not take it due to having to work the extra hours and dealing with an unruly child at the moment. I did try to negotiate and offered to work every other Saturday, but they did not allow it. For the record, a Caucasian looking girl got the job and she didn't have to work six days a week. Just had to throw it out there. I ultimately did end up being upgraded in my position when they put me in their commercial department. It's so weird, and I recall having a dream right before I began working there. My new boss, Giselle, had this bracelet on her that I liked and was interested in having it. She proceeded to take the bracelet off and tie around my wrist. The bracelet, I saw at Guess, was $30, which was the exact weekly pay raise I was getting in that department. Anywho at first, it wasn't so bad because every time you turned around our office, we were throwing parties together. When my father passed they took up a collection for me. Plus, I made two good friends, one I remain close to this day. My other friend, unfortunately, passed away. Rest in Paradise Jenn☹

As someone who specifically chose a Bachelor of Arts in order to avoid math classes now working as a credit analyst, the fancy title for collector was not my thing. The payment plans and "so-called" budgets were more complicated than a statistics class. I recall going over the information with a customer once and she said "......this is so complicated and I have a master's degree." It was on the tip of my tongue to also say that I had one as well, but I still don't get it. But knowing that I was being monitored I kept my mouth shut in order to keep my job. My fear eventually manifested into reality when the acting supervisor, Gina, asked that I remove my plant from my desk because she needed to see my face as I worked. Naturally, I refused and was given the boot by the Director, Dick, and Gina two weeks before my mother, who lay dying from cancer, passed away. It is understandable to get fired by the director who was educated but getting fired by someone who doesn't even come close to reaching the scope of my education (Gina) was an outright insult.

So once again I found myself on the opposite side of employment and applied to every top-notch job in HR that I felt I would qualify for. I spent two years out of work despite the unemployment income steadily coming in, but the bills still racked up. It got to a point that the checks stopped coming. I had to borrow against my beloved mother's treasured jewelry just as my mother used to say to turn zero to nine. When I complained to my friend/hairdresser Ella, who happened to be an ole school Haitian, she said that the reason my career/finances are in such disarray was that instead of going "right" like everyone else I went "left," meaning that while everyone else went straight to college I bullshited and had my kid, so I was forever doomed to struggle. Though I love Ella with all my heart, that's complete malarkey. There are many young women who have had children at a young age and go on to excel in life. Plus, there are lots of people who didn't start their lives perfectly but ended up doing just fine. Besides, not everyone is meant to follow the same path to get to their nirvana.

I eventually found a job that I'm still employed at till this present day. The job I have doesn't require a bachelor's degree, (I even omitted my master's degree in HR) and I don't even come close to making $40,000.00 a year. In order to keep my paycheck on the "hefty" side, I don't even take a full hour lunch, and I sometimes work extra hours to make at least 80 hours. I currently work for a non-profit women's health organization known for their abortion services as a CALL CENTER representative. At one point, I ran into someone from my church who was aware of my situation and asked if I found a job. I told her where I work and she told me it was a sin. I can't take these self-righteous Bible thumping people, you find them in all types of religions. Well, anyway, I set her straight and asked her which was more of a sin, remaining unemployed and unable to take care of my family, or I take this job and I'm able to get by. I failed to tell her, but I should have let her know that I applied to a Catholic organization's HR department numerous times and I never heard from them, but this place hired me almost immediately. In the past four years that I have been employed there I have tried to move up twice within my organization. I even revealed my education level, but was denied twice due to "lack of experience." Also, the irony isn't lost on me that the CEO of our organization and I share the same education level, but she's making way over six figures a year and I'm living on a pay that even my 17-year-old daughter would consider way too low. Regardless, my family and I have been living paycheck to paycheck. I recall reading somewhere online that no one who works full time should be poor. Well, my address is the only thing that makes it seem like I'm financially thriving. Even though my husband and I don't pay a mortgage (Thank GOD) we have had other huge debts we had to take care of, such as the gas and electricity bills. Both of these fell behind when my mother was sick, so they have increased and we're still making payments for balances from 2010. Since both are extremely high we've had to get on payment plans, and at times (during my unemployment and his) have had to ask our church to help us out. An aunt from my father's side has been well aware of our situation and was of assistance by allowing us to use her food stamp card once a month for vital groceries like meats and chicken. Now, our teen-age daughter is college-bound needing tutoring sessions, test fees, driver's permit, license and not to mention her clothes, makeup, and shoes. It made me feel like shit when she told me she didn't sign up for driver's education because it was a $500 fee, and I wouldn't be able to afford it. Do you know how incredibly frustrating it is knowing you have to go to work because you need the money, and the money you make is not even enough for one person let alone a family of three? Even though we make a budget, we end up going over due to the scheduled payments we make for cable, electricity, gas, and cell phones.

So to put it in perspective, I am part of a growing trend of the overeducated and underemployed, but when I went online I found out that I'm not the only one in such a situation. Many college grads take jobs temporarily at Starbucks, Best Buy, and other places just to make do. But what do you do when temporary becomes permanent despite ongoing effort? (i.e. me) Some just decide to go into a whole new line of work despite being college educated. Ella's son, Byron, graduated with a degree in criminology and went as far as six months without finding a permanent job, so his mother got him to get his CDL license and he now works for the bus company making well over $25 an hour which is way more than I make. As far as my student loans are concerned I owe over $100,000 for degrees that never paid off, and I have had to file over and over for financial hardship to keep them at bay while the interest accrues. Now before the violins break out I do need to admit that despite our financial circumstances, we have been on vacations from 2011 till 2014 twice to Vegas at the luxurious Aria Resort, darling daughter has a Macbook Air, and since I am the self-proclaimed stiletto queen I do have quite an impressive collection of not only shoes but clothes and some jewelry. I need to thank GOD that as a tall woman I married an average height dude or fun size one, otherwise, I'd be going crazy trying to get the expensive ass and unattainable (as for right now) "red bottoms." I try not to deny myself when it comes to looking good, but I'm really not able to buy the things I want when I want them, which sucks balls. I mean due to tax refunds, insurance, unclaimed funds, personal injury lawsuits, and renting my basement illegally out we've been able to at times stay halfway afloat, but it isn't enough. One day, I was complaining again to Ella, (don't you think I should stop) and her response was that GOD has given me what I need in order to survive, the rest is just overindulgences. Overindulgences apply when you're an overeater and you devour a chocolate cake, an alcoholic and go on a binge, or a sex addict and participate in a nonstop orgy. Not for someone who is trying to live life and support a family having to stretch leftover in their bank account of $72.24, and make it last till payday which isn't for another week. Being able to properly take care of one's family shouldn't have to be a luxury, especially if you sacrificed and worked hard for your education.

Growing up we were told that those who have no education wouldn't make it in the world, well thanks to reality TV ,Instagram, and entertainers period that's changed. I'm gonna single out rappers because they more or less usually have only a high school diploma, GED, or nothing at all. Plus, my father always said that they usually end up broke with nothing, which some obviously haven't. There are a lot of people making bank. Do I begrudge them of that? Not really, I mean I'm all for someone getting their come up on and doing what they do and getting money, but I can't help but feel like I was cheated. I recently saw something on Facebook that really hit it on the nail for me, "Black Excellence is not just for the Educated." Now, do I look down on education, absolutely not? But I am sick to death of hearing that the only way you can succeed in life is with a college education when there are way too many examples contrary to that. I do understand why as Black people we push our young to be educated having had it denied to us for so long, but I have come to the realization that it's about pursuing what YOU love and what YOU want. Not everyone is meant to have a college education, so why push someone in that direction if they feel that it's not for them. This is why I tell my daughters to do what they love, not what they think will make me or anyone else happy.

When I was little, I told my father that I was going to be a fashion designer but he insisted that it wasn't a serious career, and I couldn't pursue it. Fashion is a trillion dollar business that employs millions of people. I've always loved clothes and fashion. I remember videotaping Elsa Klensch on CNN at the fashion shows in Paris, and watching *Dynasty* with my mother to see what Alexis Morrell, Carrington Colby Dexter Rowan would be wearing. Around 2005, I became fascinated with the Juicy Couture line and I took a class through the Learning Annex about starting your own t-shirt line. I started to have an idea about starting my own line revolving around the word "Bombshell." I always love the 40s and 50s era in the movies of old Hollywood glamour, and the pin up model look. The full figured voluptuous ladies who were all women and didn't conceal it. I wanted to incorporate another word with the letter B and go from there. Such as Blonde Bombshell, Brunette Bombshell, Black Bombshell, and for the kids Baby Bombshell. When I discussed my idea with the lecturer he told me it was good, but I needed a logo to associate it with. Stuck and bewildered, I wasn't sure what to use as my logo. I thought about a Coca-Cola bottle thinking it was shaped like the hourglass figure of a woman, but quickly rejected it when I was told by my attorney that I would be sued by Coca-Cola for using their image. He suggested using a bomb image, but I immediately shut that down especially in this day and age of terrorism. Hell, I won't even wear my shirts at the airport for fear of causing panic on the plane. I half-heartedly thought of a guitar, but I felt it wasn't right. While lying down looking into my closet the answer came to me in the form of the many shoes I had. I would use a stiletto to symbolize my line. Excitedly, I met with a graphic designer who brought my vision of a logo to life. The stiletto wrapped up in the B of the word Bombshell and that was how B-a-Bombshell was born. But starting a line was anything but easy, and didn't produce the overnight success that I thought it would. But like most things in life you learn by trial and error. After my father passed away, I decided to fully go in and do any and everything I had in order to get my line off the ground, and me running to the bank. I've opened a business bank account, filed my business as a corporation, filed for a copyright, spent $500 (when I wasn't working) for a party to meet and network with some "it" people, spent countless amount of money ordering shirts, paid someone to construct a website that I never used, advertised for models on craigslist and did three different photo-shoots, trusted a 'photographer" who my friend knew who took over 100s of pictures and he provided like 20, and the list goes on and on. Even though I'm still working on getting it going, I've realized that when it comes to starting a business there are a couple of things I've learned. One of such is that there isn't a foolproof plan for success. What works for one person won't necessarily work for another. Not everyone has you or your business's best interest at heart, so be leery especially when you're shelling out your dough, and finally, you've got to push yourself and make it happen.

With everything that's happened, I've come to two realizations.. One; having a college degree doesn't guarantee success, hell it doesn't even assure a sufficient life. As I mentioned earlier, I know I'm not the only one in this situation. Whether it's the economy or just the change in times, there really isn't anything like job stability anymore. Two; you should really do what makes you happy, especially nowadays with the Kardashian/reality TV/Instagram life of turning nothing into something… "Job security is just an illusion so you might as well do what you love."

RELATIONSHIPS

I've only had two significant relationships in my life thus far. Both relationships have produced my daughters. Before my first relationship, I was so eager to have a boyfriend that I took anyone that came my way. I met my first daughter's father when I was an 18-year-old freshman at NYIT. College was a big change for me and I didn't know where to start. Even though I told everyone I wanted to be a news anchorwoman I was nowhere near serious, so I decided to focus on meeting guys and partying. I met Hakeem through my friend Monique. In fact, he was her younger cousin, so he was younger than I since Monique and I were of the same age. My mother used to say that I had two phases, either I was in the nursing home because I dated much older guys, or I was in the pediatrician's office. The age thing wouldn't have been so bad, but physically we were different as well. He was 5'6' and I'm 5'7.5 not including the big hur[4] . He was a street dude with braids that stood up straight wearing baggy clothes, and I was a girlie girl who looked and dressed the part. Hakeem was an aspiring rapper/Dj and I started to date him on the rebound. I was messing around with his friend, and I hooked up with him as a way of getting back at his friend who was doing me wrong.

At first, my relationship with Hakeem was nothing serious, but after some time it grew into something more. I'm one of those girls that the more and more I spend time around someone my heart starts to get into it. Plus, I enjoyed hanging with him and his friends. It was the golden era of hip hop back then, where every get-together was like Kid and Play's *House Party*, rhymes were spit dropping seeds of knowledge[5] . This knowledge of self was a stimulating factor for me. These guys were following the teachings of the Ansar Allah Islam, and they were telling me these concepts of GOD and man that I never dreamed of. That GOD/Jesus was Black and all the people that I grew up learning about in the Bible were all Black. They were pro-Black talking about Black is

---

[4] hur-hair
[5] seeds of knowledge- knowledge of self as Black people

beautiful, the darker the better, nappy hair was good, and that we as a Black people were the chosen ones and whites were the devil. For a girl who was raised to believe in a blonde haired blue eyed Jesus who had recently graduated from a lily-white school where she was made to feel inferior, this was the spark necessary to ignite the fire. I felt uplifted, encouraged, and strengthened. I accepted their doctrine and was sharing my new-found knowledge. I told a white friend from high school that Jesus was Black and she responded, "If I was Black I'd think Jesus was too (SMH)." My mother didn't like what I had to say, and even predicted the inevitable by stating that I should just cover myself up and put on the white veil and all, and get it over with. I justified that just because I believed it didn't have to impact me to that extent.

I was so over my head with Hakeem that I didn't flinch or bat an eyelash when he questioned whether or not I was an evil spirit due to my first name. The Imam wrote a book stating that there were names that were associated with evil entities like Damian, Evelyn, and Jacqueline. He asked me to repeat something in Arabic to the extent of "Get thee behind me Satan in the name of GOD" to prove I was indeed normal; that definitely wasn't a good sign

Warning #1. Another part which I would say was not really a warning but a deal-breaker for any young woman reading this is birthdays and holidays. He told me he didn't believe in them because why should one day be celebrated when every day is a celebration. Ladies if you ever hear this bullshit run, I repeat do not walk but run from such men. My papa always went out of his way to celebrate birthdays and holidays for my mother and myself. I had a birthday party every year till I was 16, and got Valentine's Day chocolate from him till I was married. So, if you're used to that type of treatment make sure you find someone who will adhere to it.

Warning #2 came when I drove him to cut the hair of his friend/ rapper who would eventually help launch Hakeem and his group and was verbally berated by said rapper, but Hakeem didn't come to my defense, not one bit. Wanna B Down and MC Smooth were two non-Black rappers who were successful because they rhymed about Black culture and knowledge of self. Since they provided the platform for Hakeem's group to be introduced they had to play nice to make sure they made it. So, they basically kissed their asses till they did. Regarding MC Smooth, I have nothing but nice thoughts and kind words for him. Whatever limited interaction I had with him was pleasant if not nonchalant. Wanna B Down on the other hand was not so nice. From my eye-opening experience and what I've heard about him later, he's a misogynistic, attention-seeking hole of an ass. I know you're probably saying why didn't I say anything to defend myself, well let's see I was young, dumb, and I believed that in order to be a good girlfriend I had to make sacrifices at my expense of course. So another piece of advice I offer is that if someone disrespects you in front of your man & he doesn't have the balls to defend you then you have to defend your BLESSED self, and know that no amount of dick is worth any disrespect.

My third and final warning would be regarding sex as in most relationships. I was a virgin and I wanted to remain one so I did everything (well almost everything), but the big hole in one. I always wished to be in a relationship with someone for at least a year before I gave up my virginity. Despite being younger than me, Hakeem was more experienced and was accustomed to relationships or hookups where sex was always on the table. Since I wasn't providing the good stuff he started complaining and pressuring me to give it up. He made the analogy of our non-sexual relationship to a job. He said if you're at a job and you're working hard, and despite the fact that you do your job you are not getting a raise, what would you do? He said that if he didn't get his raise he would have to look for another job. So basically he was telling me that he would find someone who would put out. I didn't give it up right away, but I eventually did lose my virginity to him. I shared this scenario with my younger daughter and she told me that I was stupid to have allowed that to influence my decision. Since I was an over-anxious person I wanted to make sure I did everything right, so I went to Family Planning and got on the pill, got foam and condoms. I remember the first time, I felt like my heart was beating from my throat, I was so nervous. Because we were always in my car whenever we were together, I wanted to make sure we did the deed in a bed, and this led me to losing my virginity at a mutual friend's house during one of our house parties. After that, we were always in my car until Monique, who was with us one day, provided a $25 gift for the motel. From then on we were in the motel even if it meant me paying, which I did the majority of the time. Now I know that was a really dumb move on my part and there is no excuse, but I felt overly compassionate for him. Here, he was this young guy with no real parental guidance trying to make it on his own. Meanwhile, I was a pampered princess who had everything going for herself and couldn't see it. I guess it was what you would call Black upper-class guilt.

Our relationship seemed to be okay for a while. On our one year anniversary, we got together in the motel that he paid for and presented me with a 14k gold bracelet; I was on cloud nine. As his rap group started to get noticed things started to change, meaning that they were making money. My friends said that I needed to benefit from this as well by comparing me to his brother's girlfriend, stating that he gets her nails and hair done for her as well as buying her clothes. Now remember you're dealing with a Black girl with a guilt complex, so I never felt he should get those things for me. Hell to this day, I don't think a man should do that. I even specifically told my daughter that she should never have a man pay for her hair, nails, or clothes because to me it looks like a low-class mentality. Make sure you do that for yourself because now that I think about it you're making yourself look good for you first and no one else. Let the church say Amen. Then my friends pushed me to go to his first video shoot. He mentioned it to me but never invited me or told me to go, so since I grew up with etiquette and thought I shouldn't go. Plus, I wanted to show that I was an authentic girlfriend and that I loved him for him, and I was not trying to get anything out of him. But my friends hounded me and hounded me till I finally went; the whole crew went. I mean it was a big deal when you're young, and someone you know is making a music video. His brother's girlfriend was there of course, and she was front and center featured in the video. I sat back like everyone else and watched until one pertinent moment of a scene involving the rappers and their "girlfriends" in a restaurant. Well since his brother had his girl, Hakeem should have had me as well. Also, I need to mention that the girl that portrayed his girlfriend was very fair-skinned with blondish hair and blue eyes. To be precise she was damn near white which was total hypocrisy with the pro-Black philosophy that they had adopted. I was his girlfriend, so I felt rightfully angry and walked out with my friends crying hysterically. I went home and for the first time, I refused his phone calls that weekend.

We eventually made up and moved forward, but as I mentioned earlier he was rising in fame, so with money came other girls which also became an issue too. Being young and dumb I never thought he would cheat on me because in my opinion, how could he cheat on me? I was the best thing for him. I was tall, sexy, and had real hair which was always my thing. Growing up in the late 80s and 90s, weaves were starting to be a big thing but not for protective styling. Weaves were used to attain lengths and styles. Everywhere I went people would make a big deal about my hair, so I used to think it gave me an edge up and used that to justify whether or not he would cheat on me. I know that type of thinking is crazy, but that was my position at the time. As I have grown older I have come to realize that when it comes to cheating for men "pussy has no age or face." Ironically the young lady who provided me with that philosophy became my friend through Hakeem. She was the girlfriend to his best friend, Alphonso, so he felt since we were both studying the Islam doctrine we should become friends. At first, I didn't really feel Nakeisha since she was more hood than I ever could be, plus she was asking me questions about our sex life but eventually, we became real good friends. She became my ace boon coon, and we were like frick and frack. Now stay with me y'all I know it seems like I'm rambling, but I promise all these will become aligned; just read on. So, as we became more and more involved in the doctrine things started to change and we accepted it; like changing the way we dressed. I've always been a body-conscious girl and I loved showing my figure, but since I converted and was down with the cause I decided to follow the code for a Muslim woman and became humble. Meaning my hair had to be covered at times and I wore clothes to disguise the fact that I had a shape. As my mother predicted, I eventually wore the Islamic garb of white whenever I was around them to show how dedicated I was. Also, I had to be submissive to my mate meaning that he would treat me any way he wanted. They, him and Alphonso, started this thing whereby if we said something that was considered disrespectful or non-virtuous they would flick us in the mouth. Fucking crazy right grown-ass young women submitting to young men who didn't even put a ring on it right let alone provide for us, but it was our truth. We even had to ask them permission if we could go to a pool party for girls only, and I remember to this day how they brought up the scripture of David viewing Bathsheba while bathing, noting how she enticed him to confirm that there wouldn't be any men there.

Things started to get more and more strenuous since they started becoming more serious in the deen[6] . Our time together now involved serving and cooking for our men. Every time we got together we would end up studying into the late hours early morning hours, so we ended up making breakfast. To this day, I hate the smell of Pillsbury cinnamon rolls. Since as a good Muslim wife we had to drop everything to cater to our men, and GOD forbid you didn't you would never hear the end of it. With that type of attitude looming over my head, I bumped into a fellow member of Islam and shared with him the knowledge and even gave him a ride in my car that "my papa" bought for me and invited him to the "bait[7] " since it had become the spot for all members to unite. Well, at some point Alphonso and Nakeisha broke up, and I assume to get back in his good graces she shared this information about this Muslim fellow so I knowing 1 +1=2 knew he would share this with my mate. So, to beat him to the punch I told him what had happened. He

---

[6] deen- religion

[7] bait-another word for the community of "Islam" where we studied, practiced our religion, and eventually lived in ; if broken down properly they used this to entice us as prey☺

broke up with me and made it seem like it was all my fault. Unfortunately, I don't recall how we got back together but we did, and it was from that reunion we moved full speed ahead and moved into the "bait" full time. Since he was my mate and had to provide for me I would have to ask him for money whenever I needed to buy something, and no matter what the amount I would have to explain why I needed it. Like if I wanted a dollar, I would have to tell him what it was meant for.

The pressure of living this way would eventually get to us and we were fighting more and more. The only bright spot of hope then was when I became pregnant. Since in our deen, you were somehow exalted if you were having a baby, but as I grew in my pregnancy I started noticing that he and the doctrine were far from ideal. I kept telling him that I needed to get away from this place and go home because I was under so much stress and it wasn't good for me or the baby, but he turned a deaf ear. The fighting translated among friends as well. Nakeisha and I were at odds. In fact, she made it clear to me that she knew something about Hakeem that would cause me to miscarry if she told me. The only information that came to mind was that she must have known that at some point he had cheated on me. I didn't let my mind go there because I honestly didn't have the energy for it. I told myself that I would find out once I gave birth to my baby. Well, I eventually went back home, and even though my father forbade me to have contact with him, I still saw him. Despite the fact that I was now home, the pressure from him didn't stop. He continued to make me feel accountable for his life. There was trouble within the rap group and he started to see that the commune we were in wasn't what he thought it would be. Since I still felt responsible for his well-being, I let him take my car for a couple of days while I was home. How my father didn't explode from the BS excuse I gave him, I'll never know. As I started to recuperate mentally and physically at home, I also started to distance myself from Hakeem little by little. In fact, it was my mother who started to talk to me day by day about my relationship and helped me see that things weren't good. The real eye-opener was when I was nine months pregnant he called and told me that he wanted me to go to the Department of Social Services and tell them I have nowhere to stay and that they would provide me with an apartment but I'm not gonna live there, instead, he would. As I felt my heart beat rapidly from the rage I heard myself say something I never said before to him "NO" and started yelling back and forth, and eventually hanging up. That was what eventually sealed the coffin of our relationship. A week later, I gave birth to our daughter and he did show up at the hospital. When I went home he came to visit, and it was then I told him I no longer wanted to be in a relationship with him. He became very emotional to the point of tears, but I couldn't be moved by that because of the many tears that I had shed. Once it was official that we broke up, Nakeisha called and told me that he cheated on me with both her friends and some other random girls. In fact, he had gotten one of Nakeisha's friends pregnant, and the only reason she didn't carry the pregnancy to term was that she miscarried. So not only was he violating our relationship, but he was also violating my health by sleeping with random ass girls without protection.

After the revelation of the indiscretions in our relationship, I was even more determined to stay single. However, Hakeem was not down with the program and decided he wanted to get back together, so he continued to try staying in my life as my boyfriend. The very last time I saw him the baby was about a month old. We actually had a nice time together. I remember he even made up a nice little rhyme for her. While we went downstairs to eat, my mother stayed upstairs to watch the baby. She immediately called me upstairs to let me know that while she was moving his coat she felt something very heavy, and when she looked in his pocket she found a machete. She clearly told me that he had to go right then and there. So as my cousin drove him to the train station my mother told me that since he was vulnerable with the breakup he might go postal and attack me, the baby, and himself so, he could not come back. Even though she mentioned this, I didn't think that could happen until New Year's Eve. He called screaming and crying that someone was trying to kill him. I eventually found out that around the time of our breakup he was robbed, or someone attempted to rob him by pointing a gun to his face at the train station. That's why he carried the machete, but his behavior now was due to him taking acid and also tripping. I finally learned that the rap group had broken up and it was just him and his brother, there were issues with the label. Plus, the realization of the falsehood of the doctrine he followed due to our experience, and the situation with me made everything overwhelming for him. Though I don't condone the use of drugs, I can't say I was surprised. Emotionally, he was very fragile, and as I mentioned earlier he was basically on his own. Unfortunately, he chose a route that he couldn't handle and got in way over his head. Since he was obviously bugging, I decided not to allow him to see the baby. I had to look out for her best interest and I wanted to make sure she was safe. He would continue to call me babbling back and forth talking about getting married, so I humored him so as not to entice or excite him any further. But after a while, I got sick and tired of pacifying him and I wanted to share my true feelings. Having had a baby three months earlier I still had raging hormones, sleepless nights from a newborn, dealing with the shame of being an unwed mother in my household, and still trying to make heads or tails of my experience in the commune. I started thinking a lot about everything and was blaming him for putting me in this horrible situation. Did I forget to mention that the girls he was messing with he had them in my presence when we were together, and also insulted me in front of one of them? Or the time after we shared an intimate moment I mentioned the video shoot and how angry I was, and I mentioned how his friend comforted me and I said something to the effect of how sweet he was. He told me in all seriousness "keep talking bitch." I began to wish him ill and shared my thoughts with my mother who told me I shouldn't think like that since I ultimately made my decision. Another thing my mother told me was to never ever accept female friends your boyfriend/husband suggests for me.

On April 22, 1993, I went out like any other normal day during the evening. I received the phone call that changed my life. Hakeem was involved in a car accident, and it didn't look like he would make it. I know this is what everyone says when they get bad news, but I literally went numb. I could not believe this was actually happening. At first, I tried to distance myself from it, but then I realized I was way too involved. The whole night was spent on the phone in order to find out what was going on. Exhausted from the stress, I tried to go to sleep. I remember waking up in the middle of the night to the sound of Anita Baker's "Angel" on the radio thinking to myself that he had passed on. The next morning I awoke to hear my mother on the phone downstairs, so I tiptoed into her room and picked up the receiver to hear a conversation between her and my godmother telling her not to let me go to the funeral. My mother came upstairs and officially informed me that someone had called in the morning to let me know he was gone. I was inconsolable with grief as I tried to hold on to my baby. The phone was ringing off the hook as friends were calling to see how I was. I eventually got a call from Hakeem's family who wanted to see the baby. I took her to see her family as they tried to console themselves with the one extension of his life. I refused to attend the wake seeing that it would be way too much for me. The thought that someone I ate with, slept with, was intimate with, and had a child with would be laid out in a casket was more than overwhelming. Instead, I attended the funeral with my mother. On April 28th, the day my daughter turned five months her father was laid to rest. Many people from his childhood friends, friends from the bait, and record company were in attendance. I remember seeing Wanna B Down there holding a rose looking very solemn. That still didn't stop me from thinking I would love to slap the taste out of his mouth. Repressed anger and valium are not a good mix. Speaking of slapping the one friend I was seeing before Hakeem was giving me the evil eye. Apparently, his friends were aware of the situation and some felt that I had pushed him to this point since I wouldn't allow him to see the baby. His death deeply affected me. I remember I had a dream about him being alive again and waking up with a strong urge to call the cemetery to see how he was. Absafuckingloutely crazy. When death leaves its mark the reactions make no sense. Everywhere I went I brought him up and now sanctified him. I recall sharing my story with the ladies at the hair salon, telling them how he was my first and one woman replied, but he won't be your last.

My parents had to go to a medical conference on a Caribbean cruise, and with everything that was going on my mother didn't want me to stay behind so she made sure my daughter and I went to Miami and stayed with my relatives. During that time, I went clubbing with my cousins and I recall going outside for some fresh air and seeing a couple kissing, which instantly stirred the thoughts of Hakeem and I. I started getting and accepting male attention for the first time in three years. It was fun for a while, but it still didn't stop my unhealthy preoccupation. When I got back to New York, school started in the fall and I tried to put my attention on that. But my mind was overwhelmed with memories and thoughts. The " Anniversary" song from Tony, Toni, Tone had come out around that time which coincidentally was around the time we would have celebrated ours. My mother used to say that the way you forget one man was to get under another. It had been a year since I had sex with someone, so I changed my demeanor becoming a little more aggressive, and made it my mission to find a guy. I eventually did something I've never done before, something very crazy. I met a young guy at school and made arrangements the next day to have sex. It was way too bold, but I wanted to erase the memories that I carried plus I had my physical needs that needed to be met. The one thing I remember and cringe as I write this was his rancid hot ass breath on my face as he lay on top of me. Plus, it was just dry sex, no foreplay or kissing whatsoever. You think that would have stopped me, but I ended up having one more encounter with him. My philosophy was something better than nothing.

January 1994, I started talking to a guy I met on New Year's Eve in a club. He was older and seemed okay. He wanted to have a relationship, but I just wanted something physical. He turned into a stalker and was somewhat of a dullard, so that had to end. Despite moving full speed ahead with my sex life, thoughts of Hakeem remained a constant factor in my mind. The last dude I also hooked up with at a club had a girlfriend which didn't bother me in the slightest. I figured since I was cheated on, I might as well be the cheatee. Despite my helping ole boy cheat, I still had standards to maintain, like the time he asked me to accompany him to his girl's job stating he would introduce me as a friend, I outright refused. I didn't mind sneaking around, but I wouldn't be flaunting it in someone's face as it was done to me. That situation lasted for about 6 months till I realized that this behavior wasn't good for me (i.e. broken condoms + no condoms = pregnancy scares/HIV testing.) Mentally, I wasn't the type of girl that could wham bam and accept a thank you, ma'am. I recall looking in my bathroom mirror telling myself I deserved better, and lo and behold I would meet the man who would become my husband.

Hubby and I met on August 18, 1995, at a pool party which my former friend, Natalie, had right by my home. To this day, whenever we pass by the house I usually tell my younger daughter, look, that's where mommy met daddy to her annoyance. Originally, I wasn't supposed to be in New York. I was supposed to be in Miami on vacay to meet up with a guy I had met from one of my previous vacations out there. We talked on the phone weekly, and as our time came closer to meet fate intervened and I never heard from him. When I first arrived at the pool party it was just getting started, so I went to see a good friend at my job and hung out for a bit. As I returned, the many cars in the driveway signaled to me that it was in full swing. Natalie's cousin, Marjorie, had asked me to bring back some cigarettes for her, so since she was in the pool I had to pass two guys to my left in order to bring it to her. As I gave her the ciggies, I turned around and saw hubby. I walked away to socialize with some other people, and while I was talking hubby came up from behind with his friend and looked me dead in the eye. I stopped mid-sentence, distracted by his stare. There was another guy there at the party that I shared a slight flirtatious with. I don't recall his name, but to this day for us, he goes by Brian McKnight. He was a tall dark chocolate brotha who made it pretty clear he wanted to have sex. Ironically, it was he that provided the courage for me to talk to hubby. He asked if I saw anything I wanted outside, and I said yes, he said I suggest you go out there before someone else takes it. I walked out determined to talk to hubby, and I made small talk with him and his friend. Eventually, as the night passed we ended up talking just us two. I found out he was Haitian and had a daughter just like me. By the end of the night, as the party wined down, we remained the only two guests outside talking. We exchanged numbers, my beeper, and kissed lightly on the mouth. I remember he said he was really glad he met me. I went home that night sharing with my mother how I met this cute Haitian guy, giving her his last name. My mother said she definitely knew his family as they were very well known in the elite of Haitian Society. Everybody knows everybody on that island. All you have to do is give the last name and you get the whole life story. I met this one guy once at a Haitian restaurant trying to talk to me and shared his name with my mother telling her he had a flat face. She said oh yeah she did know the family, and they do have pancake-flat faces. ☺

That weekend we saw each other again since Natalie decided to do another get-together. This one was more family-oriented, so I brought my daughter. Hubby and I spent most of the day together and shared our first real kiss. We were in the car and my daughter was asleep in her car seat. When I shared that scenario with my younger daughter, she said I acted like a THOT[8] . Even my male cousin back then questioned me as to why I was moving so fast. I decided to slow things down, and when we met again I had my first official date. I'm going to quote Terry Mcmillan's *Waiting to Exhale* 'white girls date, we (Black girls) don't date" we basically hook up or chill. Growing up, my father took my mother & I out to dinner at various locations on Sundays, so when I grew up and dated, I wouldn't be so impressed or wouldn't know how to act. Despite being shown how a man should treat a woman (thanks to books, TV shows, movies, and more importantly my father), I went out with "boys" whose idea of going out was Mickey D's or White Castles, which I usually paid for. This time would be different. On our first date, we went to a Haitian restaurant and I ordered the most expensive entrée, although not intentionally but because conch is a rarity and a great delight. After our date, we went our separate ways. We continued to do this for about a month. At the same time, I was seeing another guy I met at school. He was younger (I had a pattern huh) but tall, so I liked the fact that I could wear heels with him. It bothered me that I couldn't

---

[8] THOT-THAT HOE OVER THERE

freely wear heels with hubby since he's 5 '9' , making me more like a tower over him. But like my mother used to say 'everyone's the same height in bed' ☺.

Back then, I was supposed to be going to school and focusing on my studies, so dating was a definite no-no. Since I had a part-time job, I basically lied and said I was either at work or school. It got to a point that I was juggling the two guys during the week. I started to gravitate towards hubby since we actually talked and had a good time, plus he made me laugh. He had the 3Hs; Haitian, Handsome, and Humorous. As we got closer I started visiting his place. Did I forget to mention he had his own place and didn't live with his mother? Things were looking real good and got even better when he revealed that he was starting to fall in love with me. His revelation put me in an unfamiliar and uncomfortable position. Here I was for the first time not having just a physical relationship, and not trying to force a relationship. It was rare that the guy made this gesture towards me. I had to think about my feelings cause I didn't want to say it because he did, or it was expected I wanted to make sure it was genuine. The next time we saw each other, we told each other how we felt and began our serious relationship. This time things were much different, he asked for my job address so he could send me flowers (which I'm still waiting for☹), gifts were shared on the holidays,our first Easter he got a Easter basket for my daughter, and whenever I left his place he would accompany me home since the drive home was long and dark, hubby was and still is a gentleman. When it rains he'll take off the coat from his back to cover my much-treasured hair. He actually introduced me to the concept of making love because whenever I mentioned sex, he said anyone could have sex but when we finally did become intimate we would be making love. We waited till New Year's Eve to become physical. We went to Times Square to watch the ball drop and then went to a hotel. I know it sounds funny, but the same feeling I had when I first lost my virginity; my heart beating in my throat, was the same one I had when we made love for the first time. Afterward, I met his extended family and mother, he met my mother, and for the first time, I shared with my father the details of my relationship. Now pops being ole school wanted to know if he went to college, I don't recall how I maneuvered it but I made it work. Hubby had a "good job," his own place which he eventually gave me the key to, and a car. To me that was what was important, plus he supported me in finishing school and getting my degree. On Mother's Day 1996, he came to the house bearing roses for me and met my father for the first time. I felt like I was the luckiest girl in the world, but that feeling eventually passed when we had our first fight a few weeks later. Memorial Day weekend was coming up and he told me he used to go every weekend to Virginia Beach for the holiday. Well, this time he told me he wanted to spend that weekend with me. Memorial weekend wasn't a big deal for me, but since he mentioned spending it together I was cool with it. Well, three days before he called to tell me he was going to the VA I recall he asked if I was angry, and I lied and said I was fine. Eventually, I let him know I was pissed and I refused to take his calls. Now, I'm one of those girls who doesn't have a problem with her man/boyfriend /hubby going on vacay with his friends just like he shouldn't have a problem when I go with my friends, but the whole point was that he made a big deal about us spending time together and therefore lied about it. We eventually started talking and he came to the house to apologize, but he dropped a line that I would constantly hear from his mouth, "I'm a good looking guy I can have anyone I want."

Problem #1: I don't remember my response, but I took it to mean that he was out of my league and I should feel lucky that he was with me. I would be lying if I said that his comment didn't affect me. It most certainly did, but I'll get into that when I discuss my self-esteem. But despite his thoughtless remark our relationship continued to grow.

He started talking about marriage. Almost every conversation would include when we get married.

I graduated from college in May 1997, and he was a big part of the celebration again showing up with red roses. After graduation, we traveled to FL and stayed at my parents' condo. My father gave him the keys directly. I recall telling my mother how shocked I was when he did that, she said that the damage (the child) was done and there was no point in defending a "wasted" virginity. When we got back to New York his mother told me about the engagement ring, so I knew the proposal was coming soon. He proposed shortly and this time I cried tears of joy. On November 20th, 1997, I got married in the house, a civil ceremony. Now, even though I was down for a big ass wedding my mother was a precautionary pessimist who wanted to make sure that before they spent a dime the groom would show up. She had heard too many tales about the groom running away, or not showing up the day of the wedding. Right before the ceremony, I remember thinking to myself 'look how good GOD is!' Who would have thought five years ago my life would turn out like this? I had my degree, the love, and support of my family, a healthy beautiful little girl, and now I was about to marry the man I loved. My uncle was into real estate at the time and had an apartment he had considered giving us as long as we paid the maintenance fee of $500 monthly. Something to that effect didn't work out, so we decided to stay with my parents indefinitely. Now, I know this doesn't sound or look good to be living with your family as a newly married couple, but I wasn't ready to move from them after my one-time horrible experience away from home. Plus, I took the apartment thing not working out as a sign. Also, his mother encouraged him to stay with us away from the "bad influence" of his friends. His mother encouraged a lot of things including the conception of our daughter. Hubby had an identical twin brother who was killed in a motorcycle accident when he was 21 years old, so my mother-in-law is overly concerned about her living son's well-being. At the time there was a custody issue regarding his daughter, and his mother's solution was for me to have a baby. Her thinking was that he would be too occupied with a baby to focus on the circumstances. I know this sounds totally simplistic because having one child doesn't make you forget another, but since I had no real focus or job I decided why not. Unlike my other pregnancy, I didn't focus on it or pray for it, we simply stopped using contraceptives and I thought whatever will happen will happen. Well, the rabbit died and we were expecting right before the religious wedding, which was a real bitch because I had very bad morning sickness. Plus, I was spotting and was told I had an 80%

chance of carrying the baby to term. Due to the fact, I was put on immediate bed rest which of course meant no intimacy. Since I was always sick and couldn't eat, I was in a foul mood. Hubby wasn't used to me like that, plus he wasn't getting any so it was affecting him as well. One day we were in Queens and I asked him to stop and get me some Haitian bread he stopped right in front of the bakery where the pigeons were walking back and forth, so I being full fledged of my phobia refused to get out of the car feigning I was tired and asked him to get it. He got out of the car complaining and came back still complaining, and at one point he said I needed to get off my lazy ass. Hello! I'm fucking pregnant with your child which is affecting me to this extent, I started yelling back at him and I proceeded to take the bread and smush him in the face. He stopped the car and got out, then I begged him to come back but he refused, so I cursed him out and drove off.

Problem# 2: Well, despite my flying hysterics and telling my mother in a fit of rage I was calling off the wedding, we were wed on June 14th, 1998. Since I was already pregnant we didn't have much of a honeymoon, we just went down to Fort Lauderdale for three weeks. When we returned, we adjusted to life as impending parents.

Problem # 3: This occurred while we were out shopping for maternity wear. Since I wasn't working at the time, hubby was the sole supporter and he let me know how he felt about it while we were in Bloomingdale's. I was trying to find the all in one maternity outfit which I believe at the time was around $100 or so, but he said it was expensive. I said well, I like nice things. You need to like working then, he responded plainly. You see what he said here to me: his big-bellied pregnant wife; this is the reason to this day whenever I school my daughters I tell them to make sure they are not with a man that insists they work, as well as don't be with a man who forbids you from working.

Soon after, I gave birth to my second daughter with my husband by my side as I always imagined and dreamed. To this day, I sit and think back to her birth because it was one of the only times I feel I had my dream come true. I truly regret that we didn't film it or take pictures. I wish camera phones were around then. Hubby held one leg open while I held the other, and he was able to see firsthand as she came out. As they put her in my arms, I still recall his smile as he shook the doctor's hand and thanked him. My family felt complete and we started to move forward towards what I hoped would be better things. I started working full time and contributed financially to our family. Now, since I had two kids to take care of, hubby started to get neglectful in the couple part of our relationship. He stopped taking me out one on one, and treated me like "in house booty," meaning he didn't have to make any effort since I was always there. It got to a point that even my mother mentioned something about how he wasn't' trying when she heard us arguing about it. I eventually stopped begging him to take me out and started to hang out with girlfriends from work which caused even more problems not just in my marriage, but the entire household. You see, ole school Haitians believe in a patriarchal society where the man can have his fun, while the woman stays at home and takes care of the kids. So, since I decided to go out and leave my kids, who were under great supervision with my parents, I was the bad one. My parents, particularly my mother venerated hubby because he married me as the tainted single unwed mother. So, hubby milked the situation to his advantage. In fact, he would take advantage of a lot of things: my love, my family's love for me, and my naivety of marital roles. Because of this my bad temper would ignite when I've had enough, or things didn't go my way, or the way I thought they should be. Therefore, initiating a lot of physical fighting between the two of us. But I can't take the blame for all of our fights. Hubby is just as responsible, if not more due to the fact that we've had more than our share of issues which has affected our marriage to the point of separation.

Hubby and I have been married for almost 20 years now. There have been some good times, bad times, and worst times. In the first 10 years of our marriage, we definitely were on different paths and grew apart, but the following years brought us closer. I mean we've dealt with the death of both my parents, his father's, the loss of an unborn child, a wayward child, unemployment, fucked up finances, and pending foreclosure. What I've learned from all this mess is that life is very unpredictable, and when you're young and in love, you can't even fathom anything going wrong. You see/feel love and think it will conquer all. I recall reading in a magazine sometime after I was married that states there are 20 important questions you and your future fiance need to ask yourselves before getting married and I wish I had seen that article or been in the frame of mind to adhere to it. I think a lot of things could have been avoided or better planned out. Another thing I realized is that just because a man is 'a good looking guy" isn't the end-all and be all. I can honestly say that I purposely sought hubby because he was attractive. I once showed a male friend a picture of my youngest daughter and he said, "Oh you just wanted a pretty baby." Like my mother used to say, my daughter has good taste. She took her father's face, and her mother's "good" hair. I mean Hakeem wasn't ugly at all, but he wasn't presentable in "society." Just imagine my mother's reaction when she first met him. Any Haitian that's ever seen *I Love You Anne* knows that braids on a guy or "spaghetti head"is something ole school Haitians don't tolerate. Plus, he was as he's stated in his own words, a hood. So that didn't help. Hubby's a bad boy as well (as you can see I have a type), but he knows when to turn it on, and being that we're Haitian he knows what's acceptable and what's not. By marrying hubby, I made up for the shame and disaster I caused my family. However, good looks without meeting your role and responsibility as a man mean nothing. Whenever hubby repeated these words which would be pretty, often my parents on separate occasions, my hairdresser, and girlfriend Ella would say the phrase in creole "Bel garcon pa voueye nan mache." Meaning a good looking guy doesn't translate when there are bills to be paid and mouths to be fed. Plus, I know now that I bring a lot to the table as well. I'm educated, well versed, I'm the only child of a physician, and I don't look too bad if I do say so myself. I mean if it wasn't for me, we wouldn't be living in this affluent ass neighborhood. Boo yah. The final lesson I've come to realize is that sometimes as women, we tend to think that since we've been hurt the next one will be better or treat us better. Well, maybe it's not only for the guy to treat you better but for you to see that you deserve better. Let's face it, we're human, so we shouldn't put all our hopes and expectations on the next person. We have to take responsibility for ourselves and decide what we want. Maybe it is not about the next guy showing you what you deserve, but you deciding and responding to what you want and won't tolerate.

GEORGIA

"I'm a very good mother and I take care of my child," my daughter said as she left her then 18-months-old son in my care and went on with her life. Her life consists of eviction for nonpayment, dealing with a recently paroled baby father, Child Protective Services, and I can't fail to mention being a dope fiend hooker/stripper. Most people will ask how I'm able to repeat this so calmly, well the answer is simple it has unfortunately become part of my life.

Every parent wants what's best for their child, and I'm no different. In fact, as a mother, I went through hell and back to make sure she'd be better, but she rather do as she pleases. You see, my daughter was diagnosed as a narcissistic personality at 16. A disorder that can't be cured, it involves being self-centered, manipulative, demanding, lack of empathy, and thrill-seeking lifestyle. Science states that genetics and environment play a part in narcissistic development, well we might as well start at the beginning.

My pregnancy with Georgia was a bit complicated. At the time, I was living in a commune and as a woman, in the "Islamic" faith I wanted to fulfill my potential by being a wife and mother. So, I prayed and fasted to get "seeded," which was the term we used back then for pregnancy. I remember being so happy when I found out I was pregnant. I even asked the clinician to write 'pregnant' on her Rx pad so I could share it with my boyfriend. He was away on business and I was eager to share the news upon his return. When he did come back, we met at our weekly meeting and sat together as couples were allowed to. I passed him the pregnancy confirmation paper, and he gave me a half-grin and I was ecstatic. During the meeting, it was even announced of our impending parenthood, and I couldn't have been more thrilled. Never mind, we didn't have any money or lived in squalor, we were bringing another being into the world of Islam. But with the reality of pregnancy came morning sickness and excessive tiredness which affected my duties within the "bait" . It made me an easy target for my fellow female roommates who called me shiftless and lazy. Once that came to play as well as not being able to eat properly when my appetite came back, I decided to leave for my sake and especially the baby's sake. But how was I supposed to go back home when I had left in such disarray, and now come back pregnant. I remember going back and forth with my mother who knew the situation and finally got my father involved in it. When he heard me crying and blurted out I'm pregnant, his words still make me wanna weep as I write this were "come home." I never forgot the day I left. I had been talking to my good friend, Aisha, about leaving for some time. She had warned me that if I stay I would be risking my life as well as the unborn child. Aisha and her boyfriend both came by like they had to tell me something had happened to my mother after a good five minutes of fake convo at the local Chinese spot, I ran upstairs to the apartment with fake tears to explain my situation, and bounced never looking back. When I got home to my parents I ate like I had never seen food before. Puzzled and disturbed by my behavior, my father brought me to the family room to discuss my predicament. I told him I was five months pregnant and he nearly leaped off the couch. Pops probably thought we still had some time to try and get the situation taken care of, but clearly, I was much further along than he expected. After a detailed conversation and witnessing the hurt and damage I had done, I was allowed to stay. I tried not to let my pregnancy be a burden to my family, so I continued to go to the free clinic at Nassau County Medical Center. The clinic is nowhere near a private doctor's office where you come in for your scheduled appointment and meet your OB/Gyn, go quietly over your tests/details, and then go about your day. No, this involved having to show up at 8:30 am and not being seen till around 11 am, bringing in a sample of your urine, and being surrounded by a number of pregnant females which included prisoners in the neighboring correctional facility. Not a pretty picture huh. During my last visit there, the clinician on staff didn't realize she needed to give me an internal exam. She kept stating that she was behind, and needed to finish so I had to remind her. Since she was in such a hurry she ended up bruising my cervix, and I started bleeding lightly. She tried to brush it off as normal but when I shared what happened with my mother, she said it wasn't. This prompted my mother to lobby for my father to add me to their insurance. From then on I was seen by a private doctor. So, in essence, I ended up being totally dependent on my parents for everything. In the next four months of my pregnancy, my emotions went from a naivety of happiness to an awakening of anger, frustration, and shame. I didn't fully realize what I had gotten myself into, especially as the daughter of a prominent Haitian-American citizen coming home pregnant without a husband and a proper education was like a death sentence. When my parents had visitors my mother would tell me to go upstairs and hide so no one could see my growing girth. A close friend of theirs came over and told me to my face that I've ruined my life. My father came home one day from work and found me crying. I was one month away from delivery and it hit me like a ton of bricks that I was gonna be responsible for a new little life.

November 28th, 1992 I gave birth to my daughter, Georgia Marie, weighing in at 6lbs 1 oz with my mother by my side. My boyfriend and her father was still in the picture, but his role was limited as that was one of the conditions of my father. Actually, my father didn't want him in the picture at all. Since he was providing for me and mine food, room, and board, I obliged. Particularly when it came to the birth certification registration. My father told me I had to put her father as unknown, which thank goodness in the hospital I was given a choice whether or not to add the father's name, which I chose not to.

Returning home after her birth I settled in the role of the young mother. My cousin suggested that I let my parents raise my daughter, while I go away to college so that I could have a much better chance of getting my life back on track. With tears in my eyes, I looked at the sleeping infant, and wilfully answered no. I wanted to be home with my baby and not miss one moment. I stayed home for almost a year bonding with my daughter before I went back to school full time. Since my mother was a stay at home type she provided the love, warmth, and guidance in my absence as well as in my presence. For my father, I felt like I was watching what it must have been like with me. It was like he had another daughter all over. All of the anger and disappointment went right out the window when he was with her. Her father's family was not really involved until his untimely death. Once that occurred they made an effort to be in her life for about a few months or so, and then without warning, they stopped calling us. I never tried to pursue them, and just blew it off. She had so much love and affection from my family, them not being involved was irrelevant. As time went by, Georgia, and I both grew up together. Her first tooth, step, words, and first birthday. Her first day in Pre K, I cried as I realized that my baby girl was growing up. Her first day of kindergarten, she wet her pants and I was there in a flash to bring her clothes. I knew all the words to every *Aladdin* and Cind-Nella, how she normally pronounces *Cinderella* when she was three. Thanks to her to this day whenever I see *Hey Arnold* or *Rugrats*, I see her little face. She was the first person I hugged when I graduated with my bachelor's. We were always together as a mother and daughter team. Any man who was interested in me would have to take us both. I became seriously involved with my future husband when she was three years old and married when she was five years old. She witnessed both my civil ceremony and was my ring bearer in my formal religious one. When my husband moved in, the dynamics shifted and it was no longer "Ta," "Papa," "Coe," my cousin who lived with us, Mommy but now Mommy's husband. At first, I let her call him by his first name but then as I grew big with my second child I thought it would be more appropriate if she called him "Daddy." Once my second daughter was born she experienced new baby angst. The past five years were all about her, so it was only natural she experienced some jealousy. Plus, it wasn't just "daddy" but a new daddy and new baby with mommy. The best moment I recall was my first weekend at home from the hospital, my newborn was crying and my hubby put her to lie down between us as I was in and out of consciousness from the nightly feedings. Georgia stood by the door looking in on this vision of a family. I remember she looked so troubled wanting to come in and not wanting to come in. My husband called her in gently and made her lie in between the both of us with the newborn lying in Georgia's arms. It was the sweetest most genuine moment I witnessed. To me, it was his way of letting her know she was part of our little family. Unfortunately, her relationship with my hubby became seriously strained to say the least.It's no secret that

Haitians believe in disciplining their children with physical punishment in the form of hitting. That hitting usually involves a belt, but as any Haitian kid will tell you it doesn't have to be a belt. It could be a shoe, wooden spoon, comb, heck even a plastic bottle. Hubby seemed to think he could discipline and punish Georgia as he could our daughter. But here's the problem when you live with your parents, who otherwise raised your daughter for the first five years, they provide their opinion and therefore continue to mold and shape her whether it be good or bad. My mother who continued to share a very close relationship with Georgia would always tell her that he wasn't her father, so he had no rights. The only problem there was that my parents, particularly my mother, felt she had more say with her. Even when hubby and I were first engaged and were in the process of getting an apartment (which apparently didn't happen), my mother said Georgia would stay with her and see me on the weekends. You see, most ole school Haitians view step-parents as infiltrators and try to keep the child as far away as possible.

My mother particularly took her role as grandma to another level. My mother grew up in Haiti without a father. My grandfather had done "something" that forced him to leave his wife with two kids, and pregnant with a third. She always narrated how she suffered growing up without her father, so Georgia being an illegitimate child and without a father always got what she wanted. She deliberately spoiled my daughter due to her own insecurities while growing up. She wanted her to be able to get anything she wanted and not want for anything. So, whenever I couldn't provide something there was my mother with her credit cards. She was her protectress, her confidante, and most definitely her biggest enabler.

I didn't really start to see any real changes in her personality until she was around 12 years old. She became more materialistic, headstrong, and selfish. Having been a psych major I witnessed her change and got her some counseling, but it really didn't help. By the time she was 14, she was well on her way to being out of control. Her freshman year in high school she was as they say 'lit' . She rarely went to class and was basically with her friends. Her report card was full of the F's, or Incompletes. All year I was going back and forth to her school dealing with her attitude problem. When she was going into middle school I told her all along not to take any crap from anyone. Looking back at my formative years I regretted not being told to stand up for myself, so I always to this day insist my kids don't take any shit from anyone. Georgia took hers to the next level and was argumentative with school mates as well as faculty. I recall telling her that she can either be a smart ass and an A+ student, or be an F student and keep her mouth shut, but she couldn't be a double negative. I realized I needed to get some help, so after 14 years out of sheer desperation, I contacted her father's family and explained the situation. After a visit to the ATL to see what could be done, I realized they weren't going to be of any help. By the end of her freshman year, the school psychologist took note and recommended her going to a school within the area that would be more suited to her behavior. I was in total agreement, but he informed me that she would have to decide. I was outraged at how a 15-year minor child has the right to decide where she would go to school. I thought it was ridiculous. So after visiting the school, Georgia walked out of the tour and the school psychologist asked what was wrong? She proceeded to tell him that the school looked dirty and the kids looked, excuse me for saying this, "retarded" and she didn't belong there. I just stood there with my "I told you so" kind of look.

She continued to stay within her high school but was eventually kicked out due to a physical altercation involving a student and a teacher. During that time she went buck wild. From police officers coming to my home, sneaking out at night while the whole household was asleep, running away from home, to physical altercations between myself and her, stealing or borrowing my mother's credit cards without permission, and ordering whatever her heart desired. My mother tried to stop the deliveries once by refusing them. Georgia, being the clever smart ass, told them that my mother, who spoke English with an obvious accent, was the maid and to disregard her. My mother used to say "Li pa pè Dieu ou Diable," meaning she wasn't scared of GOD or the Devil. I went to Family Court and filed a P.I.N.S, Person in Need of Supervision, a petition against her since punishment and threats weren't working. The big warning came when I found out that she was driving our neighbor's brand new Jaguar. Her friend,Stacy, the neighbor's daughter, would steal the keys and they both would go joyriding. This all came to head when the car keys went missing and she had them in her possession. I panicked thinking that if they were found on her it would mean a lot of legal problems. So, we got rid of them and I started to get serious about finding a boot camp type school for her. But most were expensive and once I read some of the reviews they scared me even more. Thanks to a relative who experienced the same thing, I ended up enrolling her at Miracle Meadows in Salem, West Virginia. The only problem that remained was how to get her down there. Since she was well aware of my entrepreneurial ambitions, my friend "other Monique" (I have two friends named Monique both born in April , both Black, and best friends so we call one other Monique to not mix them up) and I tricked her by telling her we were going to Maryland to meet with a famous music producer who was interested in financing my clothing line. Since we added a celebrity to the game we knew there was no way she would say no. Before we left on Friday night, she went out and didn't return till the morning. We left around 11 am and drove the eight hours straight to West Virginia. That was before daylight savings so when we arrived it was pitch black out. Salem is like the buttcrack of West Virginia, a small town inhabited by less than 2000 people and still flashes the confederate flag, so you can just imagine as three Black women it's not a great place to be in the middle of the night. Plus, having gotten hooked on to the *Wrong Turn* movies which are supposedly set in West Virginia about a family of inbred hillbilly cannibals, I was even more terrified. While we drove my friend's car her gas light came on and I told her we needed to find gas ASAP, but she said we had at least another 30 miles till we'd have to worry. I told her we need to get gas now before we end up being someone's dinner. We got to a gas station and I immediately called the headmaster and asked if he could meet us, which he did. The school turns out was located way out in the woods somewhat on a mountain. When we got there, Georgia went into full panic and tried to run, fortunately there were school officials and students who were able to subdue her. We went into a conference room, and I told her that as her mother I could not continue to watch her destroy herself. I was putting her here so she could make a change for the better and give her a chance at her life. She cried of course, but I stayed firm. I didn't break down till my friend and I got to the hotel in the neighboring town. The night attendant, Tom, saw me in tears as I broke down because I was so upset about leaving my daughter at the school. He comforted me by assuring that I was doing the right thing, and everything would work out fine. While I slept in, other Monique went and got everything Georgia needed for her new school and we delivered it to her on our last visit before we left. I still recall her in the van with her schoolmates waving goodbye to me. Driving home to New York I cried over and over to the other Monique asking what kind of mother leaves her daughter with strangers not knowing what could happen. Other Monique reassured me that I was doing the right thing. When I got home I tried to get back to a normal life of dealing with my bullshit job and raising my youngest Cassie, who was nine at the time. When two days had passed I tried calling to see how she was. The school's policy is that the students are not allowed to make or receive phone calls for two weeks, so I was on pins and needles waiting to hear her voice. I needed to know she was okay, and I finally spoke to her after week two. From then on she called me weekly and I also received letters. I recall one phone call when she told me that she went for her first full doctor's exam as a "woman" and we were discussing it. She said it was okay, but wished I was there with her during her examination. Even though my mother tolerated her to some extent, she could see through her manipulations.She told me not to fall for her sad tale and asked me, did Georgia wish I was there when she lost her virginity????

Financially speaking the school wasn't much of a stretch for some people, but for someone making $30,000 a year $2000 a month was a lot to swallow. I had used a good portion of my tax refund to pay the upfront fees and tuition, but after the first month, I was stumped. Thankfully, my mother's friend was aware of the situation and she gave us the money to continue with her education. Even though I was able to keep her in the school it still didn't keep my mind from running and asking whether or not she was being treated well. Was she being abused physically and/ or sexually? As a mother sending her minor child at the mercy of adults who you don't know is very scary not knowing what can be happening, but also knowing you put her in that situation makes it even scarier. I was crying almost all the time. I didn't get any peace until my father passed away in August 2008. When my father died, the school told me they would bring Georgia back with two escorts for the traveling cost of $500 dollars. There were many family members who stated that I should have left her in school and not spent the money, but I refused to let her miss the funeral of the only real father she ever had. Once she came back, I saw that she looked fine. Even my mother commented that she had the image of a skeleton-like, or a malnourished young woman facing us but instead she came back looking like she gained a couple of pounds. The escorts stated they needed to keep a watch over her since she was brand new to the program, so they accompanied us to get her some clothes for the funeral. They also slept in the same room as her to make sure she didn't try anything. After the funeral took place, she tried to manipulate me into removing her from the school, but I held steadfast. As I mentioned earlier, once I saw her and the staff within my home I was able to get some peace and know she was being properly taken care of. So our lives went on without papa until around October when I was unable to make payments toward her tuition. The school worked with me for a while but then, I finally received a warning from the headmaster that if I didn't pay the tuition I owed they would have to send her back home. So, in order to give my daughter the fighting chance at changing for the better, I closed my 401k from a former employer and handed the school around $8,000. The money from the 401k would only hold the school off for a little while, but I needed a permanent solution. Solace came from my therapist who told me that I could sue my public school in order for them to cover the tuition and provide me back the money I had spent. Once I further investigated and met with an attorney, I moved forward.

We continued to visit her at the school for Thanksgiving/Birthday during that time, and other holiday long weekends. It was required that families visit their children at least three times a year to help with the program of getting them back home. The family weekends would include meeting with teachers to discuss progress and group therapy. It was at one of the family weekends that she and my hubby had a breakthrough in their relationship, and put their past to rest. Hubby was very encouraging and said we needed to do what we had to make sure she came back home. Even when we held a mass to commemorate the one year anniversary of my father's death, it was hubby who insisted she came back and paid for her flight to and from home for the weekend. Everything seemed calm for a while and I thought Georgia was changing for the better. Then she came home for Christmas vacation and tried to manipulate her stay into a permanent one. She got her wish two months later when she came back home indefinitely due to the fact that the public school officials needed to have her come back to interview and evaluate her. It was then that after various questions, the psychologist diagnosed her as a narcissistic personality. She stated Georgia was manipulative, self-centered with an extreme sense of entitlement. The one person she truly had empathy for was my mother of course. Once she came home, she went back little by little to her old ways of going out and staying out late and reuniting with her friends. Even though she no longer was a student at Half Hollow Hills, she attended the school prom with what would have been her graduating class. Despite the fact that she was acting up, my mother fully funded her prom expenses. It was during that time that my mother was diagnosed with thyroid cancer, and we were told nothing else could be done to save her; she declined right before our eyes. Since she was terminal they sent her home with us. The only person who assisted me was Georgia, which I realized must have been very difficult for her. To see your once strong viable mother figure now helpless, wasn't an easy pill to swallow. She helped me bathe her, change her, and feed her. My mother couldn't even communicate with us. This was hard to watch as a grown-ass woman let alone a teenager. One day she went shopping with her friends and while I was home struggling to take care of my mother, I got a call from Macy's telling me my daughter was arrested for shoplifting. I was absolutely livid. How could she do this after everything we were going through? In a way I kinda understood, though I'm not excusing it, she was lashing in response to what was going on.

My mother eventually died October 17th, 2010 with Georgia and the caregiver we hired within the room. Another death to deal with. After the funeral, we received word from the school that they wanted to meet with us. The school board and attorneys decided to continue to support Georgia's education provided she went back to Miracle Meadows. Georgia didn't want to go back there even though it would take three more years for her to get her high school diploma if she stayed here in NY. Miss Alexa, who was director of the girl's dorm and someone I stayed in contact with, had provided a solution. She stated that she would be setting up a school in her home country of St. Lucia that would be an annex of Miracle Meadows. She agreed to take Georgia for the remaining six months. Georgia still refused to go. Even my friends used to say can you imagine spending your senior year of high school in the Caribbean?" Who would pass up something like that? Finally, after a serious discussion between hubby, Georgia, and me, she decided to go. So after getting her passport expedited and purposely missing her first flight, she finally made it there. As were the rules before I talked to her on the phone and via email, I got pics. Upon graduation, I spoke to Miss Alexa and had a lengthy convo regarding her coming back. She stated Georgia needed a lot of structure if she were to return home. If not she thought it would be best that she lives on her own. We went over the rules and guidelines with her and she came back home the following week. I was so happy she graduated and was coming home. I decided to set up a celebration for her and her friends. The next day she was out and back to her old tricks again. She'd go to parties during the week and weekends, and wouldn't be able to come home because she was drunk or high. I spoke to her several times and told her it was time to get serious. I advised her to go to school or get a job. Since I was broke, I took her to Nassau Community College to enroll in school and got an application for financial aid. She never filled them out and went the route of getting a job at the dry cleaners. Things were calm for a bit, but she continued to have issues here and there. She had quit the dry cleaners for a job at Abercrombie & Fitch, but it didn't work out as she expected, so she got back to hanging out. I could no longer tolerate this behavior especially since I had an impressive 12 year old I was raising, so I put her out hoping it would make her change. This going back & forth took place for about two months. She had come back and I told her she couldn't continue to live in the house since she was dead set on living life on her terms, so it would be best if she lived on her own. She agreed and went out that Tuesday night coming back causing a commotion. That day I told her that I couldn't have her coming in after midnight due to Cassie having to go to school, and hubby going to work. I told her it is best not to go out, or if she did come home in the morning around five or six. She came back at one am ringing the bell and shouting because I refused to let her in, so she called the cops. So much for a peaceful night. The next morning I went about my day like nothing happened.

Georgia eventually returned within a week or so with a major attitude to get the rest of her things. She did call me eventually to let me know she was traveling and was in Vegas. I thought she was just enjoying her life, not thinking twice about how she got there, or what she was up to. So much was going on in my life, dealing with my parents' premature deaths, a house I inherited with a mortgage I couldn't pay, raising a tween, being unemployed and money issues I couldn't even go there. Then one Friday while I was out she called me crying and asking me to come get her. I asked her over and over what was wrong, but she just kept crying and then hung up. I tried calling her back over and over but got no answer. So, I furiously drove home and once I got there I finally was able to reach her. I asked what had happened. She said everything was fine to disregard everything, this got me so confused and dumbfounded. I had no idea what was going on so I tried to put it to the side. Then the shit hit the fan when her friend called me and told me she was caught up with a guy who got her involved in prostitution in Denver. She even sent me the online link of my little girl selling herself. Nothing ever prepares you for this type of news. Not even in my wildest imagination did this ever cross my mind that she would degrade herself to that extent. I got in touch with the authorities in Colorado and was told that there wasn't much they could do since she was 18. They put together a plan to entice her, and then they contacted me once they had her in custody. Hubby said we needed to go down there, but since money was tight, how would we get there. I shared the news with some close family members and asked if we could borrow the funds for our trip. I also had a male cousin, who was close to her, going to be in the area asking if he could try and get in contact with her. He seemed eager at first to assist, but when it got close to crunch time he decided not to get involved due to it being "GOD'S plan" for her.

The authorities were able to get her, and I spoke to her crying my eyes out trying to convince her that she needed to stop what she was doing. She blamed me and said it was my fault, and this is what I get. I tried to bring up my father and mother, but that made her more irate. She told me to forget that she exists and said something to the effect that she was dead to me. I didn't hear from her till the following month when a friend of hers let me know that she was back in town for court. I "bumped" into her and tried again to talk some sense into her, but to no avail. We didn't speak for another six months after. When we finally did talk, she reached out to me and we made plans to meet for dinner. I was early and ecstatic to finally see my prodigal daughter. She of course showed up late, but nevertheless, I was happy to see that she was alive. I decided to apply that old adage that you can catch more flies with honey than vinegar, so I spoke calmly. I asked how she was doing. She told me she no longer was hoeing but was doing the next best thing ………..stripping. In my heart, I was like how did she end up this way, but out loud I told her that was better than before. We continued to meet every weekend for dinner for a couple of months. Each time I spoke to her and rehashed the same speech, you are still young and have your whole life ahead of you, this was just a mistake I made them too, yaada yaada, I thought it was registering until she had to have an emergency appendectomy and while I was at the hospital I found out that she had used "Molly." While she was recovering, we got to talking but as always with us, we got to arguing. She tried to use the fact that she needed to have someone take care of her while she recovered. I told her that I could not have a known drug user in my home without supervision, plus my minor child there. She refused to speak to me and I didn't see her again till her attorney contacted me. He spoke to me candidly, of course not telling me what was going on exactly but that she was in deep shit and he wanted to speak to me one on one. Hubby and I went down to the office and met with both attorneys telling us that she was involved in a lot of messed up shit due to her boyfriend/pimp. They asked if there was somewhere we could send her to some relative to get her away from everything. Even these two strangers could see that the lifestyle she had was gonna land her in jail, or in the morgue. They even mentioned that mentally something wasn't right. She showed up and I was able to speak to her. It was then that I learned that she was pregnant. As an employee of Family Planning, I have spent a lot of time discussing with young women how to make the right decision. I feel a termination is a very difficult decision and should not be taken lightly, so I wanted to be as diplomatic as possible about the situation. I told her it would be her choice but a child is a big responsibility, and I felt that she wasn't ready to have one. She and I continued to speak at one point, and she said that she realized she needed to have a termination and was upset. I told her I would go with her when she was ready. Then a few weeks later, I got the call that she decided to keep the baby. I told her I would help her whichever way I could. She sent me sonogram pictures and eventually shared it was a boy. She asked if I would throw her a baby shower, so my mother's rich friends could get her nice gifts. Same ole Georgie I thought as I tried to explain that even though I supported her having the baby it wasn't an overly joyous occasion. But she didn't get it.

While she was in the early stages of her pregnancy she had nowhere to go, so I called a close family member in FL; the aunt of the male cousin I had who was in Colorado. She's a Christian and she was well aware of the situation, so I asked if it was possible for her to stay there so that I would be sending money monthly for her and help out any way I could. I was told that she would pray on it and I never heard from them again.

Georgia wanted to come back home, but she wanted to come home on her conditions, not mine. Plus, this was what I had mentioned earlier to her that she wasn't ready for a child, she needed to have a roof over her head, food to eat, and to avoid stress at all costs. How was she going to cope if this was happening and the baby wasn't even here? By the time she was around six or seven months, she had somewhere to live permanently. There were little incidents here and there like going to the ER with her on Christmas Eve, buying and delivering food during a snowstorm, false labor, and paying for a hotel. At one point, she realized that she needed to get away and spoke to a member of her father's side of the family, and was going to move her to Atlanta. I bought the train ticket because by that time she was nine months into her pregnancy and I was gonna drive her to the station but she kept changing the date until finally she never went. A week before she went into labor, she called me asking if she could leave her unregistered car parked in front of my house. I declined her request knowing it was probably obtained illegally, she proceeded to go into her normal rage and curse me out. She said I never did anything for her and never wanted to see me. A week later she gave birth to her son via C-section. Even though she didn't want to see me, I struggled internally and decided to go to her and my grandson. The minute I laid eyes on him I ironically cried like a baby because now he was here in the flesh, and I could only begin to imagine what his life would be like. After visiting him, I went to see my daughter whose first words were, "What are you doing here? I thought I told you I didn't want to see you." As I was leaving the hospital I took my anger and frustration out on my friend, other Monique who was not taking into consideration the reality of a prostitute having a baby for her pimp boyfriend. For the next week or so, I wondered if everything was fine until my daughter called under the guise that she was looking for a pediatrician. From there I spoke to her praying that she would allow me to see my grandson, but my prayer would go unanswered. She was gonna make me pay for what she felt was not supporting her. She let me know now that she had a stable environment, and I was under no circumstances welcomed in her home. I became an emotional wreck, I wanted to see my grandson and make sure he was okay. I fed into her manipulations just so she would allow me to see him, which wouldn't happen till he was three months old. A license plate for her car was sent to my home and she needed it, so we met at a diner near her home around 11:30 pm. When I finally saw him I was overjoyed. Not only was he well taken care of and safe, but to be able to see an extension of yourself makes you feel blessed to see the next generation. During that short time, she told me that she had a full-time nanny taking care of him. She promised she would continue to allow me to see him and I believed her due to this kind gesture which of course was because she needed something from me. From that time on, I would call her and make arrangements to meet with her and she would either not answer the phone or never show up. The final straw was when she told me to meet her at the baby's pediatrician. I sped from work to make it on time to the doctor's office and waited 30 minutes till it finally hit me that she was not showing up. This cat and mouse game had to stop. I texted her that I was done and left her alone while I suffered in silence. Thanksgiving weekend, she called me yelling and screaming that I was a terrible mother and grandmother because I didn't extend an invite to her for the holiday. Any normal person would think to themselves, well I've been a flake and I never showed up, so should I expect my mother to call me let alone invite me? Not my "darling daughter." She called with entitlement and expectation in her tone as she proceeded to cuss me out and hung up.

Christmas morning, she showed up at my doorstep with her baby in tow, leaving him with me for almost six hours with half a bottle of formula and one diaper while she went to get his things so he could spend the week with me. As I chastised her lateness, she claimed she fell asleep. Thinking to myself that since she works nights, it was only normal she was tired. As I proceeded to bond with my grandson I put all that out of my mind, but it eventually caught up as I became more consistent in his life. Things like her not answering the phone when needed, her never being home according to the Spanish speaking nanny, who therefore would call or text me when the baby needed food or diapers, leaving the baby with the nanny and her family for two weeks straight without calling, and here we go, folks, dropping a dime bag of oxycontin when she picked up the baby. With that last doozy, you would think I called the authorities. Well, let me explain how they work. They have to catch her in the act, so without proof, there's nothing that could be done. Plus, they said she had all her bases covered with a nanny watching him.

Thankfully, thus far, little man has been shielded from this due to the nanny, his other grandmother, and myself, but we knew the shit would eventually hit the fan and this lifestyle my daughter is living would in time catch up to her, and it did as I stated before.

Now, my take on this shitty situation that stinks to high heaven is that there is an innocent sweet baby boy in the center of this mess who didn't ask to be born. His welfare is the utmost concern, and it is because of this that I scheduled and unscheduled time off from work, begged my 17-year-old this past summer to watch him and gave her whatever little money I had so I could go to work, turned my home into an all-out romper room, taken my money to pay for his doctor visits when he had no insurance, dealt with his unstable ass mother which has led our already combative relationship into another physical altercation and dealing with her pimp/ baby father. Not to mention I have fallen completely and madly in love with this little fella who deserves so much better than a drug-addicted prostitute mother, and habitual felon father. Speaking of my daughter, do I think she loves her child? Absolutely I do, but as a narcissist, I don't think she is capable of a selfless type of love. As far as Georgia is concerned I do love her, but I am so GODDAMN angry with her for throwing her life away. This was a child who was afforded all opportunities and just threw it all away. She grew up pampered and loved, and yes there were issues, but what family does not have their share. My mother used to say that there was a Haitian proverb that says that a mother's breasts are never too full when it comes to her children. Well, my poor little boobies are on the verge of collapsing. Whenever I see or hear of someone's child that is around Georgia's age, and making strides in their life like graduating college or following their dreams without causing problems for their families, it really makes me feel like shit and so ashamed. Even though I feel humiliated by my daughter, I refuse to take responsibility for her actions. I know some will say that children are an extension of their parents and that she's only following in my footsteps by having a baby out of wedlock, but that is not the case. Children come into this world through us and are raised by us, but in essence, they are not us. A child that does wrong does wrong out of their own choice despite their family or background. I mean, look at me despite being raised as a sheltered and spoiled daughter of a physician I did my wrong and ran off with my boyfriend, and got involved in a cult producing said daughter. But it was all me, not my mother's or father's fault. Just like GOD has given us free will, our children have free will too.

When I think about the possibilities for Georgia's life, they are endless. She could be accomplishing so much more with her life. Despite the fact that she is deeply involved I still have hope that she can turn her life around, but it's not up to me, it's up to her. So until then I tolerate, I love and I pray.

HOKEY RELIGION AND LEAVING HOME

"Were you kidnapped?" My pending obstetrician asked as I voiced my concerns for my unborn baby due to the physical and mental stress. I had endured living in a commune for seven months. "No, "I replied, "I was just stupid." During the early 90s, along with the golden age of hip hop, was the empowering black culture movement. Though these concepts and thoughts were not foreign, having been taught earlier during the 60s and 70s that they were never explicitly put out there as they were once rap became the voice of the people. Every time you turned on the radio dial songs were practically shouting that we as a people were kings and queens, the original man, and robbed of our culture and true religion. Hakeem was a strong follower of this movement and he introduced me to it. Actually, he followed the teachings of Imam Isa and was a member of the Ansaar Allah Community. They believed in the one true GOD as Allah, and that whites were devils. I recall when he told me Jesus was Black; I dead ass argued that He was white. I justified my argument with the many paintings and drawings I had seen in church and school. Like the one that hung in my mother's laundry room with His pale smooth holy illuminated face, piercing green eyes, and long straight hair. This was my Savior and Redeemer. Well, Hakeem provided me proof with the Bible itself from Revelations chapter 1 verses 14-15. Now I don't have much of a poker face, so my reaction betrayed my thoughts, and gave me something to think about. Every time I saw him, he would provide me with some additional information that made me question what I was raised to believe. Like when he told me Adam and Eve were Black again, he provided evidence from the Bible. He said that if GOD created man out of mud, which was dirt and water, what color was it? Now I know this is gonna sound cliché, but my eyes did pop out of my head. Not only was the proof in the "chocolate" pudding, so to speak, but because the evidence was under my nose the whole time and I never noticed. I began sharing my new-found knowledge with those around me, like my parents. My mother, being a conservative ole school Haitian, didn't want to hear it. My father surprised me and responded by stating that he was aware of this. He even gave me some of his own knowledge by comparing Moses to the Egyptians. Papa said that since the Egyptians were Black or dark, how then could a white Moses pass for the son of pharaoh's daughter? Since I felt like I had my papa's blessing, I divulged deeper into this way of thinking.

As my relationship with Hakeem grew, so did my dedication. Even though I responded positively and accepted some of the deen, there were some things that I couldn't accept. For instance, they didn't believe Jesus was the Son of GOD, but rather He was the son of the angel Gabriel due to the scripture verse in the King James version of Luke chapter 1 verse 28 "And the angel came in unto her, and said, Hail, thou that art highly favored, the Lord is with thee: blessed art thou among women." Their interpretation meant that the angel ejaculated inside of Mary. Another example I didn't agree with was regarding Jesus as well, stating that He was not crucified, but rather had a "double-take his place," and He escaped to another country to live the remaining years of his life preaching. Jesus was a big part of my life, and there was no way I was gonna just drop everything I believed in now. So, I combined what I believed in Islam with my Catholic upbringing. The spring of 91, my first Ramadan, the time of fasting that most Muslims partake in, was around Lent/Easter, and I did both. I gave up something that I felt was important for 40 days and fasted during the day. I remember when I went to church on Easter Sunday thinking that I could finally eat something, but then realized that was the Catholic faith not the Islamic one. I began to absorb the culture immensely and tried to emulate a good Muslim woman. Since the role of a Muslim woman was to be a good wife and mother, I decided I needed to learn how to cook. I bought a cookbook and since my mother was an excellent cook, I followed and learned from her as well. The first dish I made was lasagna and I followed it to a tee in the recipe book. I went all out and used canned tomato sauce, crushed tomatoes, and tomato paste. Not the one jar of Ragu that I currently use when I want to make it. I'm a realist and know that it tastes just as good if not better, plus ain't nobody got time for that. Anyway, I was so proud when I presented it to him. After that, I started making chicken, rice and beans, spaghetti and sausage, and lots and lots of cakes. I recall one Ramadan, all the girls put together the celebration feast and contributed a dish or two. Well, your girl here made four dishes including a cake. I wanted to show Hakeem that I would make the perfect wife for him, and mother to our kids. Speaking of kids was also a big part of the deen. Children were seen as pure beings and would be the 144,000 beings that would save us. They would be groomed and raised with Islam in their hearts. When I was little, I would always love to hold and play with my baby cousins and my mom's friend's kids. In fact, I fell head over heels in love with my mother's friend's baby boy, Jeffrey, when I was around seven. My mother said I refused to have a party for my first holy Communion unless the baby was there. So she had to have two parties, one in the day for the kids so he would be there, and one at night for the adults. I always loved babies/children; growing up, I couldn't wait to be a mother. I watched too many TV shows where the woman went into labor with her loving husband by her side and couldn't wait to experience that. When I was 15, I went on a cruise to the Bahamas with my parents and their/my friends and family. I shared a cabin with my friends. I recall saying out loud, "Can you believe that one day we'll be mothers and we'll have babies of our own?" My friend Sabine said, "Don't you want to focus on something else than being a mother? What about a career? Bingo! At 19-20, I shouldn't have been more focused on wanting to have a baby and getting married. I should have been out enjoying my youth, going to parties, meeting different people, traveling, and focusing on my goals and dreams for my future. But that was the problem. I didn't know what I wanted to do with my life. I felt like my friends had their careers mapped out going to law school or medical school, but that wasn't for me. Hell, I didn't even think college was for me, but in my family/culture and background, you could not decide not to go to college. It was the natural order in our world. As natural as breathing, eating, shitting, and sleeping, you graduate high school and go to college. Since I had no idea what I wanted to do with my life, Islam and Hakeem provided the perfect outlet for me. I had no real hopes and dreams for myself, so I invested them in my boyfriend who did. So, ladies, if you are reading this, make sure you have a dream, a plan, or a focus for yourself before you get snatched up in someone else's☺.

I remember imagining that we would live in a little house in Queens, particularly my cousin's house on Farmers, he would work and bring in the money while I would bear and raise our seven children. Yep, you read right, seven kids; six boys and one girl, like Jacob and his first and fertile wife, Leah. Now, as I mentioned, fertility since having kids was a big deal. If for some reason, you as a woman can't bear or carry your own child, then your mate could then take a second wife for that purpose. As in biblical times, the baby would be considered your baby. When we girls found out about this, Nakeisha said, "I can't imagine knowing you having sex with my mate for a baby for me." SMH ...Since that was something that would loom over our heads, I started to become obsessed about it. I decided to stop taking birth control pills and we started "raw doggin[9]" it. The first time my period was late, and we thought I was pregnant, Hakeem was totally there for me. This was what we wanted, right? One night, I remember he came over and we "accidentally" fell asleep. I started fantasizing what life would be like if I could be the stereotypical baby mother living at home with my mother while he would come and go as he pleased since my father would be "conveniently" out of the picture. My father was hardly home because he worked two jobs, so I was able to get away with a lot including having my boyfriend in the house and inappropriately falling asleep. I picture this ideal life of being big-bellied and it being okay. I pictured myself wearing beautiful maternity outfits (always a fashion maven) having my baby shower not with my friends that I grew up with, but the new friends that I had through him. Going shopping for my baby items and taking Lamaze together. At that moment, I didn't see any fights, any struggle, and any despair, just an idyllic uncomplicated situation and I would do anything to make it come true.

---

[9] raw doggin - having sex without protection

From that time on, I became fixated with getting pregnant. It obviously didn't happen like we thought, so we just kept at it, but it didn't happen soon enough. I figured maybe it was because I wasn't an official Muslim, so I made arrangements to do my "Shahada." My official conversion into Islam. Even though I didn't fully agree with some of the doctrines, I still went full speed ahead. Wearing the white garb with my face covered up, I went from Sybil, had to drop my slave name to Naima, which meant pleasant and a gift. Once I was officially converted, I thought I'd be pregnant within a heartbeat. But it still didn't happen. Then physically, I noticed I had a lot of discharge and pain in my pelvic area. Now, before I reveal my diagnosis, I will say that a lot of shit happened between Hakeem and I, but one thing he never did was burn me. Since I felt this was something that could affect my fertility in the long run, I dropped Family Planning like a bad habit and found myself a professional OB/GYN. That she was black, and a woman was a plus. Also, she specialized in Western medication as well as herbal remedies , which was an additional plus being that in the deen they wanted to stay away from medication as much as possible. She diagnosed me as having an infection that was going into my fallopian tubes and provided me with antibiotics as well as some herbal teas to help clean out my system. After that fiasco, I kept seeing her to make sure everything was good. I remember coming back from her office once and telling Hakeem she said that I was fertile as a horse (my words, not hers), just to show him I was okay. Since pregnancy was my main focus, I began to dress the part as well by wearing empire waist dresses, and around that time, baby doll tops were the rage, so I wore those a lot as well. Whenever anyone would ask or say I was "seeded" as they called it, I would bashfully grin and think from their lips to GOD's ears or rather Allah at the time.

Even though I was trying to be grown by wanting to have a baby, we still did teenage things like going to the movies, going to McDonald's, and going to parties till around the fall/winter of 1991. I don't remember word for word or how it went about, but we went from running the streets of Long Beach to getting ready to move into the "community" as they called it. Instead of our couple time together, we would now include all of us who were dedicated and disciplined. So, every get-together involved studying and praying. The fellas started hanging more and more with the exclusive members of the deen Yala and Basheesh. They would come around often and we girls agreed that they were really fine particularly, Basheesh. One time last minute and all the fellas decided we would spend the night and part of the day in the Spring Valley community. When we got there, it was a high ranch house that I, Nakeisha, and Christale stayed in, while the fellas were separated and spent the night in the house for the men. I recall when we got there, it was around midnight, and everyone was asleep. A female guided us to the nursery where we would sleep, and the three of us huddled together on the floor. Mmhm, that's right, no mattress, just some blankets if I'm not mistaken, we brought ourselves and literally made our bed. As we settled down to sleep, we started to discuss how we would make the transition from leaving our homes and the *dunya* (the world). We all mentioned how hard it would be leaving our families, but it had to be done. The next day, we awoke to the women coming into the nursery to tend to their children. We met Yala's wife Emira[10] Badra, who was in charge of the women, had two sons and was pregnant with her third. We met Yala's second wife as well since, in Islam, it's permissible for the man to take a second wife. Regardless of it being accepted, the tension was obvious between them and they did their best not to show it. The second woman in charge or the Emira's backup was Basheesh's mate, Mariyah. As expected, she was short, light skin, well Puerto Rican; so I guess the light-skin came with the territory, and long dark hair. Her most obvious features were her indented dimples that lit up her face when she smiled. She had two kids, as well a little girl around three years old named Faatina, and a baby boy between seven or eight months named Israel, plus another baby on the way. She would eventually become our Emira. As we met everyone, we watched how life went on in the bait. I recall listening to two sisters discussing their mate time. Since men and women were separated, you had to ask your respective Emir[11]/Emira's

---

[10] Emira-feminine commander, leader
[11] Emir-commander, leader

permission to spend the night with your own husband/wife. Now, the permission depended on both performances of each of the mates; the men with their peddling and the women with their chores or duties. If neither were met with what was considered suitable, then it could be denied. After we ate breakfast, we went to their weekly meeting. Like in any sales meeting, they spotlight the brothers who were bringing in the most cash. There were laughs, cheers, hugs, and lots of clapping especially as they turned their attention to us. They mentioned Hakeem and Alphonso saying something to the effect that they were aware of the "truth" since they brought their wives here. Cue the applause. I now suspect that they were going extra hard for our sake in order to show us how united and cohesive their lives were, drawing us in even more. Now, I know you all are probably thinking, 'Girl, you should have ran from this nonsense and bullshit, haven't you ever heard of a cult and communes??' Absolutely, I was well aware of Jim Jones and the People's Temple and kept comparing it to them to make sure it was not like them. But it was, and I was hooked. I don't know; religion was always a huge thing for me growing up. I always tried to make sure I was a good person and doing GOD'S will. I mean, when I was little, I read a lot of saint stories and even did everything I could to live up to the standards to become a saint till I grew up and got into guys.

Before we were moving to the community, it was made known that Hakeem and I had to get married. Men didn't have to legally marry women who weren't virgins, but those whose mates took their virginity had to legally wed. We started to look into getting married and even went to Town Hall to get the information. Around that time, Nakeisha mentioned to me to make sure I found out everything I needed to know before I took the final step with Hakeem. I didn't pay her much mind and just thought she was jealous since I was and could get married. Eventually, we found out we were considered married since he was my first. Islamic marriage consisted of presenting your mate/wife with a nose ring and some bangles like they did straight out of the Bible. Out of all the girls, I was the only one who didn't rock a nose ring. I guess I still had some of my Haitian standards and wouldn't go there. One day,

I had Nakeisha come to my house as my parents were going out. After they exchanged hellos, my parents left, and as I closed the door, my father pointed to his nose, then to her inside, and made a severe grimace. Even now, my youngest daughter will teasingly tell her grandmother that she's getting a nose ring, and my mother-in-law has a fit. In Haitian society, decent people don't get them.

The Ansaaur Allah population in Long Island was growing, but there was no home base for members to live. Alphonso rented an apartment above his father's shop and gave up his home for the sake of the deen. So, moving in came sooner than expected. The picture of Basheesh and his family moving in remains fresh in my mind till this day. Hakeem and I were sitting outside in my car talking as we watched them walking towards the bait. Basheesh and Mariyah were holding little Faatina's hand, and Mariyah carried baby Israel with his little legs on her pregnant belly. That image never left my mind thereafter because I wanted us to be exactly like that, the perfect Islamic family. We would soon find out this was anything but true.

Since I had a car, I was permitted to stay in the "*dunya*" and live at home. Many other members were moving in daily. One couple, Shaia and Zakkia moved in with their baby boy. Our good friend Pauline moved in shortly after with her mate. The women lived in the apartment and the men stayed in the basement, and EVERYONE shared the bathroom. We had our jobs mapped out for us. One girl was responsible for cleaning, one for the cooking, and one for taking care of the kids. I was the chauffeur, and I would take Mariyah whenever she needed to go. The mall, market, fabric store, and Department of Social Services. A lot of these ladies were dependent on the system and made it seem like they didn't know where the father of the children was so they could collect food stamps and financial assistance. It was a slippery slope that was, in essence, defrauding the government. So every day, I would wake up from home and go straight to the "bait" and then come home late at night to sleep. I no longer interacted with my family. I was already hooked. I'll never forget the day it became official. At one point, Emira Mariyah told me over the phone that her mate said I couldn't continue with this arrangement. She said that if I was gonna move in, I had to do it now. So, I packed my things and got ready to move. I told my mother I was leaving, and she exasperatedly told me to just go. My parents and my cousin Claude from Haiti, who was living with us for school, all sat down to dinner as the cab honked to alert me of its arrival. As soon as I got to the bait, I told Mariyah I was here permanently. She told me to iron all the brother's garbs since tonight was the night of prayer. I started to iron but began to feel dizzy at some point. At the time, I had a very bad cold and was having a hard time recovering. I was physically run down, not eating or sleeping much and running around back and forth. Anywho, I had a dizzy spell and asked one of the sisters to take over the ironing, and she did. Mariyah came into the room to check up and saw that I wasn't ironing and said, "I thought I told you to do the ironing." I explained that I wasn't feeling well. Strike one of these; controlling ass behaviors. I spent my first night participating in the night of prayer. You did 100 salats from around midnight to sunrise. If you passed gas in any way, you had to start again by washing up and starting over. I prayed that it wouldn't happen in order to show "Allah" how dedicated I was, plus I still very much wanted to be a mother and I thought that making the 100 prays straight would bring me closer to my dream.

Life in the community for me now involved taking care of the babies/kids each day. I would feed and change three baby boys and educate the two little girls. Actually, the girls started to educate me since we were supposed to be speaking Arabic, especially to the kids. Since children learn faster than adults, they already knew a lot of the vocab and taught me so I could communicate better. Looking back now, I recall coming back from grocery shopping and Faatina coming to the door and frantically telling her to leave in Arabic in front of Hakeem to show off my verbal skills and progression. SMH. Eventually, our duties usually changed or rotated especially if someone tended to leave which ultimately occured very often. Christale was the first to leave. She was around five months pregnant, and her boyfriend wasn't even living there. Her leaving affected Nakeisha particularly since they came in together. Once she left Nakeisha took out a lot of her aggression and anger on me. Since I wasn't a fighter and I was trying to emulate a virtuous woman, I tried not to engage in any argument with her. But every little thing I did would ignite her wrath on me. In fact, many of the sisters started to not get along. What do you expect when a group of friends/strangers are living together? Unlike *The Real World,* we were not put in luxury accommodations. Hell, we weren't even in working-class accommodations. We were a total of 25-30 people living in a three room one bathroom and basement apartment. The seven or eight women, three babies, and two little girls shared the two rooms above. We slept on the floor mattresses all in one room except for the babies who slept in the second room with their mothers. The second in charge, Bethuna, and her children. The Emira had her own room which she shared with her daughter and son. Even though someone cleaned every day, the apartment was less than sanitary. We had roaches and mice. One day as I was doing a nightly prayer, I stood up and as I got ready to kneel, I looked down and saw a little gray mouse right on my prayer mat. I ran right out of the room to inform everyone. I recall Zekkai telling me something to the effect of what I should have done to which I responded; do I look like someone who knows what to do when it comes to mice. I basically ratted; no pun intended ,myself out so to speak. As my mother would have said, I confirmed I had no business being there whatsoever. Most of the people who were living here had lives that I had only seen on TV like a parent in jail, sexually/physically abused, and neglectful parents. Most of the people I hung around before I went to the community came from single-parent homes while I was the only one who came from a two-parent home. Even the Emir made fun of my upbringing when he heard me on the phone with my mother discussing my father in which I called papa. He brought it up at our weekly meeting in front of everyone stating you should hear Naima when she talks "Papa Papa" all proper. I was nothing like these people, and again they showed me I had no business being there. But despite this, I still stayed even when one of the kids told me that as I slept, a roach crawled out of my hair, and I suffered severe diarrhea on a daily basis due to the sanitariness of 30 plus people sharing one toilet. Shit, again no pun intended, I was the one that provided the pep talk to the others who cried that they missed their family members and/or mother that we had to continue for the deen that would eventually change once I became pregnant. I was always big on prayer, and I did a special type of prayer to get "seeded." I fasted for seven days and did the prayer at night. Since we didn't have official mate time, Hakeem and I improvised. Despite the fact that they told me I had to leave my car home, the Emir would always ask me to get my car for a couple of days claiming we would need an extra car to go to Spring Valley which we sometimes did or travel upstate to hear the "Lamb" himself speak, which, as I knowing digress, was considered a "reward" to go and hear him speak in person. The one time I went we did not go into the great hall which was covered with columns in a gold array and all, but instead an annex with no heat in the dead of winter and watched his lecture on TV screens because the hall was full to capacity. Then after driving back home three plus hours, we ate General Tso's chicken which was the "Lamb's" favorite food, so we could only have that. To this day if I see it or hear about it I get a way about it . Real crazy and fucked up shit right, any who since I thought I was helping out, and plus whenever I wanted to still be able to see my parents, I would go get my car. My parents allowed me to take my car, and my mother would later reveal to me to make sure I was alive and well. My daughter was conceived in the back of the supermarket in the back seat of my car with Islamic hymns sung by the "Lamb " playing on my tape deck. Once it was confirmed that I was pregnant, one of the sisters told me Mariyah had said she doesn't know how and when I got seeded since I never had official mate time. She was doing a lot of trash-talking behind our backs. They say children always tell the truth, and her little Faatina would often say, "My *ummi (*means mother) doesn't like you she told me." At one point, I went to visit my parents and I got sick and went to the emergency room. I ended up spending the night at home and came back to the bait the following morning. She welcomed me back smiling as though everything was good. I later found out that when I called her to let her know I was sick, she went and talked to the other sisters about me saying "She ain't sick or she didn't go to no ER, she just wanted to stay at home."

Mariyah was a street chick from the boogie down Bronx who had a total of five children all together. She revealed to us that she had twin daughters that were with their father because she had them young, and apparently neglected them as infants and had them taken away. It seems that she left her five-months-old twin babies alone in a house with no electricity to go party. So much for the perfect Islamic mother. Even with her remaining kids, she spent as little time with them as possible. She preferred to leave them in the care of the sisters and go out instead. She gave birth to her third and final baby while she was with us. Part of our deen again involved distancing ourselves from Western Medicine and trying to be as natural as possible. So, no OB/GYN visits, or pediatricians visits for the babies/ kids. Even though she wasn't under a doctor's care she delivered at Columbia Presbyterian in the city. I was right out of the room when her daughter was born, and I cried tears of joy as I heard the baby crying. When she came back home, she spent maybe a week or so at home breastfeeding and was back out and about while her baby went straight on formula, something that was strongly discouraged within our religious dynamic. Since I felt a special bond with the baby, I took care of her. The sisters used to say she was my baby since I was always with her. One day as we took care of the babies, we provided her formula or gave her something to the extent that caused a lot of gas. As we told her when she came back, her once sunny disposition turned stormy within seconds. She could be very moody at times, not talking to anyone and doing her own thing. Also, this woman who was supposed to be our leader was illiterate as well. At one point she had to read something given from "headquarters" and she stumbled over the most basic words. We all looked at each other like "Yo this bitch can't read." I know the signs were all there, but I kept at it. Her mate wasn't any better. As I mentioned earlier, he would drive my car for what I thought was related to the deen, but little did I know he was dealing drugs/guns out of my car. We later found out Yala and Basheesh were considered top peddlers because they used the drug money to contribute to the deen. So, if he got caught and arrested my innocent hardworking father would be penalized as well since the car was registered in his name. Right after Mariyah had given birth, he dropped me and Zakkia off on Jamaica Ave to get some stuff before the baby came home. He was supposed to pick us back up, but he never showed up. We had to walk in the freezing cold a number of blocks to get public transportation to go back to the bait. As well as being sneaky, unscrupulous, underhanded, and corrupt he was quite perverse as well. Again, he dropped me and another sister off and her true blood sister came along for the "excursion." Well, this girl had on a form-fitting dress with black stockings and heels. It wasn't a totally out-there outfit, but she had a nice figure so he couldn't stop his tongue from literally hanging from his mouth. He just kept cheesing at her as she paid him no mind whatsoever. After I left the community, I eventually found out that he had propositioned Hakeem to switch mates. Hakeem tried to laugh it off, but Basheesh told him he was dead ass serious.

At one point they acquired the apartment in the next-door building. Since it was considered bigger, the women moved there, and the fellas stayed at our old place. At that time, we had additional sisters move in, one woman moved in with her three kids, and two single ladies moved in as well. The next apartment was even worse with the vermin. We had to do at least four roach bombs for the three months we were there. You could hear the mice at night as well as the daytime, and they would walk openly without worries on the stove at night. At this point, I reached a new plateau and started thinking that I needed to go. Especially since with my newfound pregnancy, I was extremely tired and nauseous. In order to get the much-needed rest, I went with Bethuna to her home in Brooklyn while she ran errands. I slept in. As my appetite started to increase so did my frustration with everything, but especially because there wasn't enough food to go around. The market was done on a daily basis, and it was dependent on how much money the brothers collected when they peddled. They handed over their money to the Emir who would then give it to the Emira, and she would either take the money herself and go to the market or give a certain amount to a sister to buy enough for everyone and do the best that she could with what was given. Zekkai used to exclusively breastfeed her baby, and one time the baby was wailing so much trying to nurse but got nothing. Zekkai had to give the baby apple juice and rice cereal mixed, and he sucked the bottle dry. She mentioned it to Basheesh who told her that there was a prayer she could do to increase her milk. Nakeisha said there's not enough food and he's talking about praying to increase your milk. Eventually with stuff like this happening Zekkai and her family left. One by one many people began to leave. Even Basheesh started to notice the once full weekly meeting where he would tell the same joke about Mariyah wanting to go to the Poconos, and he would poke her nose once met with a roar of laughter and approval after a while would be met with disdain and contempt. I begged Hakeem to let me go back home to my family, but he refused. As my pregnancy progressed, I turned to him often complaining about the conditions and stating over and over again that this was not safe for the baby. But he was steadfast and wouldn't let me leave. Now, when I say he wouldn't let me leave, he didn't have a gun to my head or threatened me physically, so I could have left anytime but it was all psychological. I was bound there by mind games and the threat of being corrupted by the "dunya" if I went back home. I reached my breaking point when I heard Hakeem say that you can't say no if the "Lamb " wanted your mate, you would have to oblige because that's the "Lamb " smiling and all. It was then it hit me that this do as I say, not do as I do philosophy was most definitely a cult. So, I plotted my getaway. I stayed in touch with my friend Aisha who was a social worker, and she was aware of everything and in contact with my mother. I wasn't sure if I would be able to go back home since I was far along in my pregnancy , so my mother was prepared to make arrangements with Aisha to find somewhere for me to go if my father wouldn't allow it. Thank GOD he didn't say no. So, Aisha came on a Sunday with her big muscular boyfriend Shawn, in case there was a problem, pretending that my mother had a heart attack and leading me into the Chinese restaurant that was on the block to talk further and throw pepper in my face to produce fake tears. I ran upstairs to tell Mariyah my tall tale and got some of my things in a trash bag and left. The minute I was in the car driving home I felt as free as the wind coming through my windows. By that time my parents had moved to an upscale neighborhood, and I was overjoyed that they allowed me to stay. The first thing I did was shed myself off those clothes and take a real shower with no roaches crawling on the toilet or tub, no women's underwear, or soiled diapers around, and definitely no one asking you when you would be finished. No, this was a clean fresh bathroom to me and as I let the water flow down, I kept telling myself I was free. As I tried to acclimate myself to my new, yet comfortable and somewhat familiar surroundings, it still wasn't over. Not only was I dealing with being home in an unsavory situation, but the effects of being in the commune were still present. My first night at home I ate like I hadn't had a real meal in a while, my parents both exchanged shocked looks at one another. During the week I went out with my mother and cousin to the nearby supermarket, I could barely keep my eyes open as I slept through the whole ride. My mother later revealed to me as she went to the market with my cousin while I stayed in the car and slept that she was crying her eyes out. What have they done to my child??? She's like a zombie!!! The sleeping was nothing compared to the fungal infection that attacked my body even months after I left. I started to have a prickly itching under my arms and a thick layer formed. My mother would have to clean the area twice a day with alcohol and spread medication in the infected area. Along with attending to me, my mother had to further attend to her home since along with my clothes in the trash bag, I brought some friends, ROACHES. My mother, who was rightfully embarrassed by this, bought the little roach traps and had them on the kitchen counter and told visitors that they were decorations. Plus, I cannot forget the weekly parking tickets from Basheesh using my car that came in the mail addressed to my father that my mother paid for without his knowledge. Those tickets must have come for a good six months straight. With the physical damage, came the emotional damage of trying to repair my relationship with my parents. My mother and I spent a night shedding tears as we discussed how much I hurt her by leaving home the way I did. My father walked in on us calmly telling me we would discuss everything together the next day.

Day by day I revealed to my mother the events that took place while I was away from home, and as we talked, I began to realize this was a cult. What Hakeem feared would happen manifested as I no longer believed, and I was pissed. Pissed that I let myself get so deeply involved and so out of control. Plus, I was angry that I was so eager to be submissive to fucking strangers who were obviously immoral and depraved. I used to fantasize running into Mariyah again where I had the upper hand and make her pay for what she did. At one point, I thought of calling social services and reporting her ASS for fraud, but my mother reminded me that since I was a mother now, I shouldn't do anything for it to come against my baby.

It's been 23 years since this nightmarish experience, and I can honestly say I really haven't given it much thought until I started writing. Do I regret it? Absolutely, I regret it with everything that I am, but out of this experience, I grew and became the woman I am today. As far as GOD is concerned, I realize that my relationship with HIM is not what I read in a book or what someone standing behind a pulpit in a church, mosque, temple, or storefront says. It's between me and my MAKER and nobody can tell me what that is. Amen

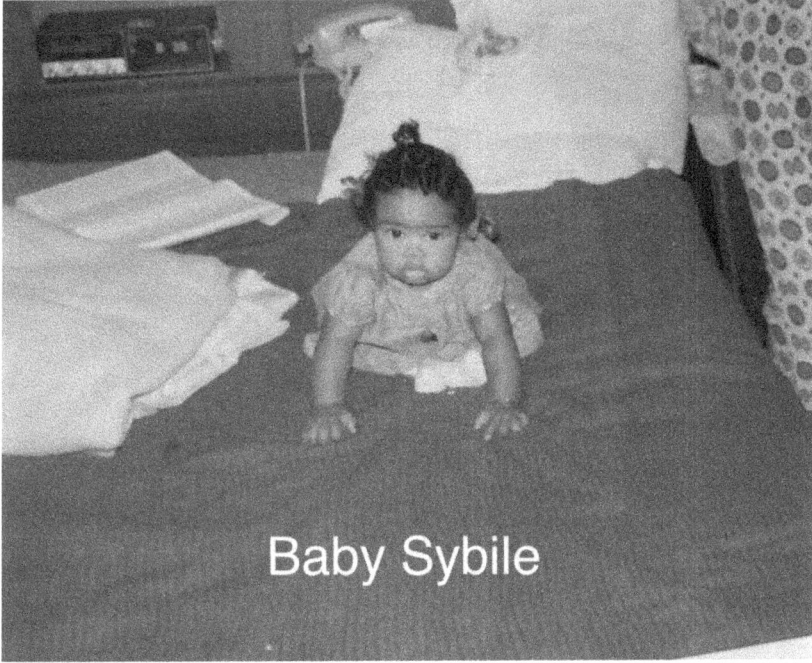

Baby Sybile

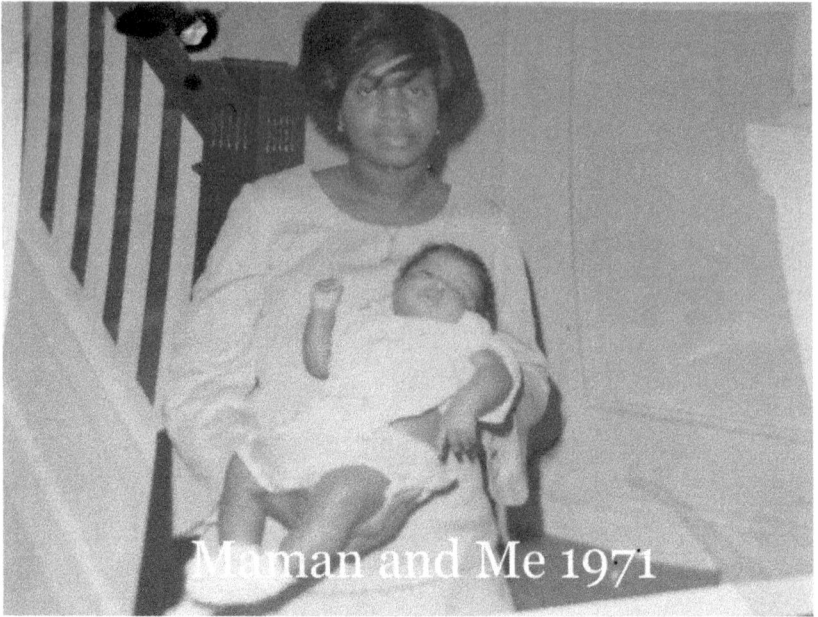

Maman and Me 1971

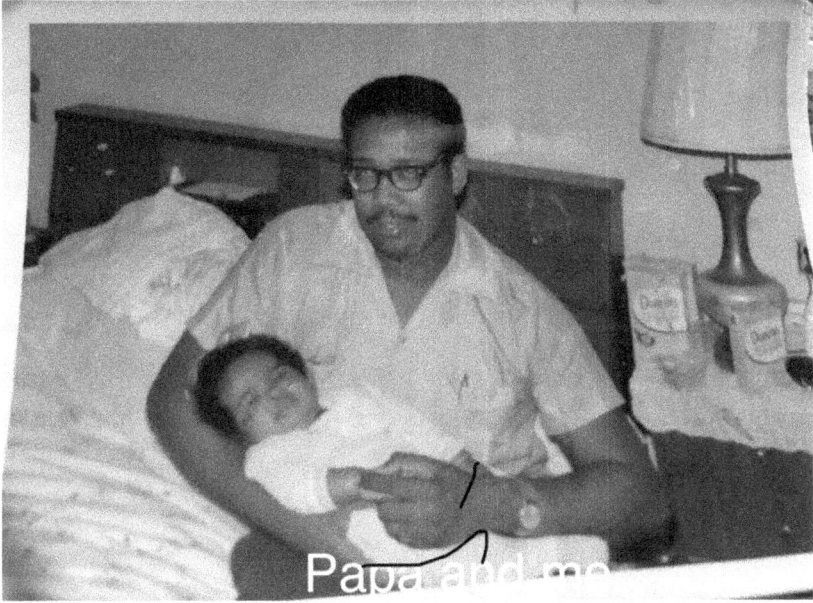

Papa and me

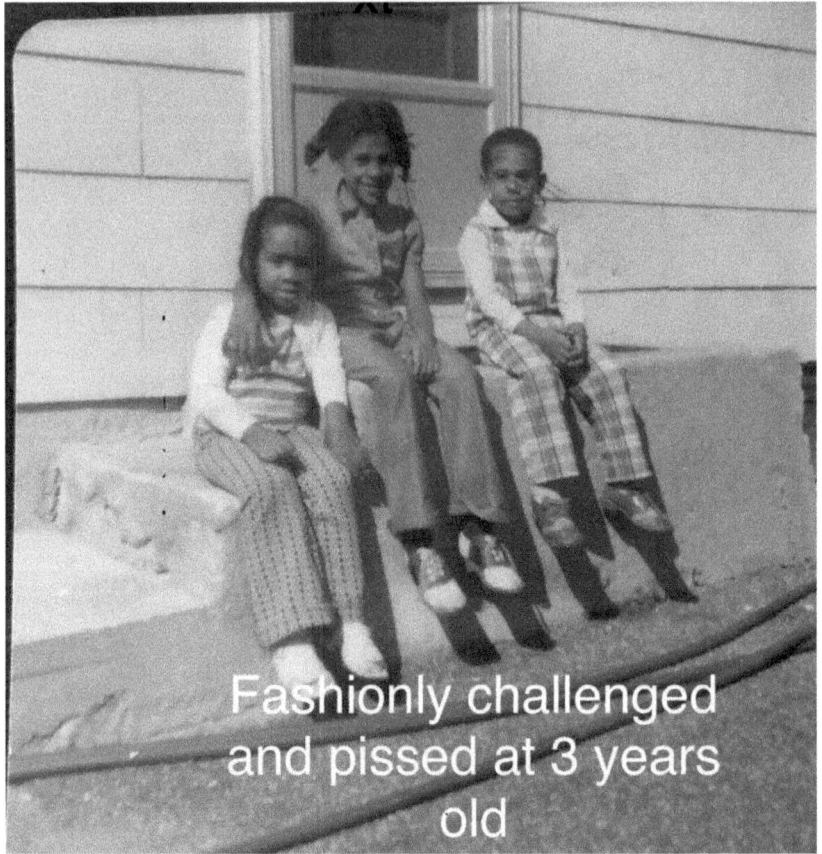

Fashionly challenged
and pissed at 3 years
old

Kindergarten

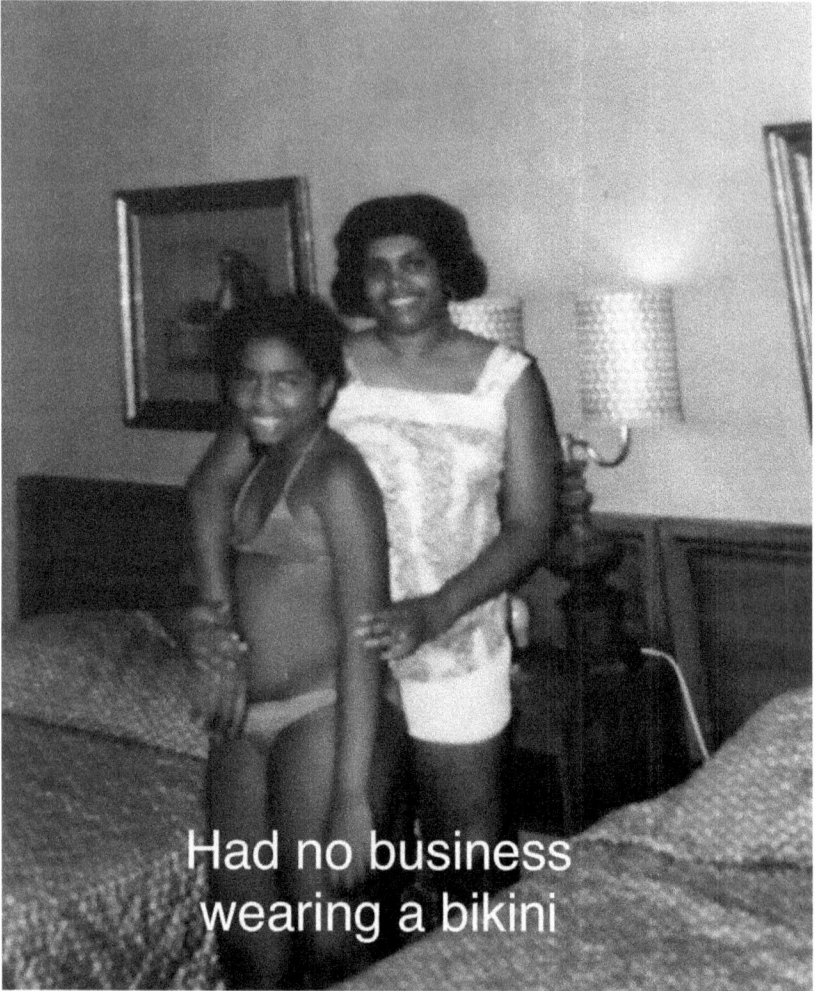

Had no business
wearing a bikini

Fat me

Sweet Sixteen

Haircut from Hell

Halloween 1988
Anna and Me

Big Hair Don't Care

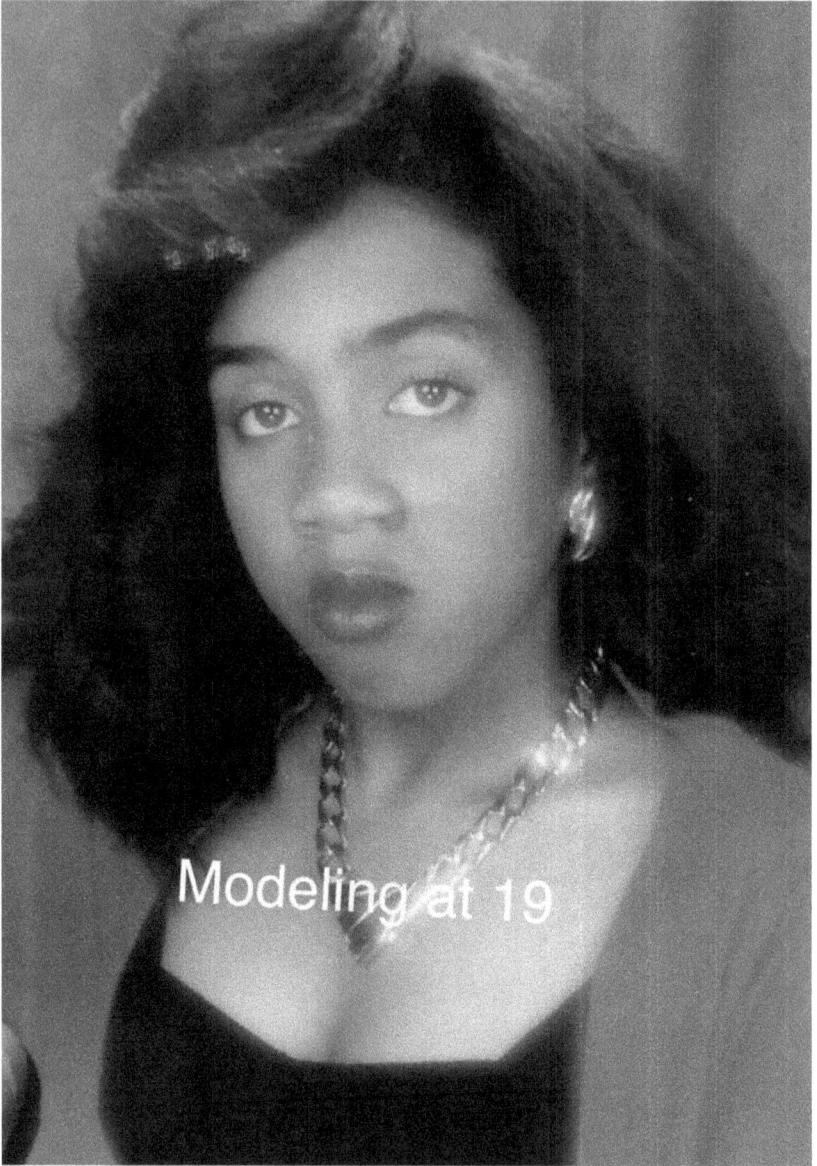
Modeling at 19

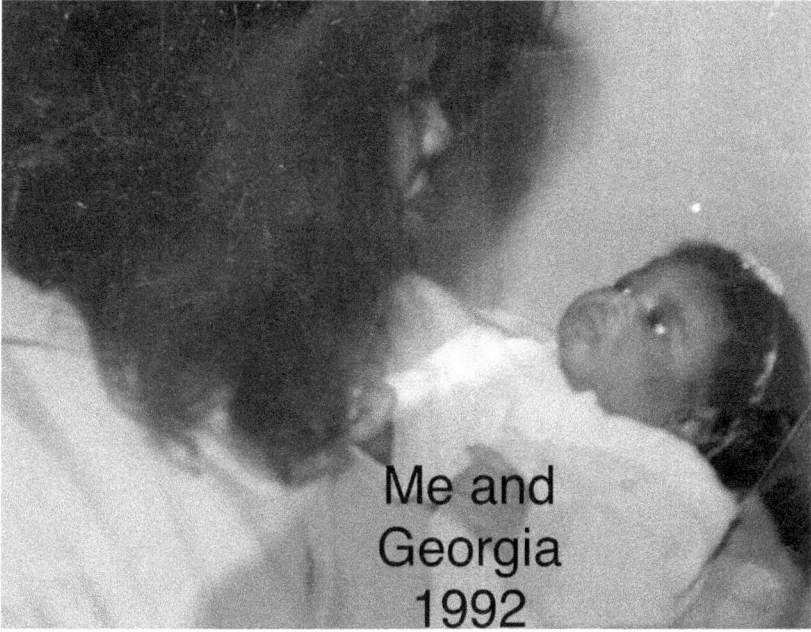

Me and
Georgia
1992

Bachelors
of Arts

Miami hubby
to be and me
1997

Civil Ceremony 1997

Forever
Daddy's girl

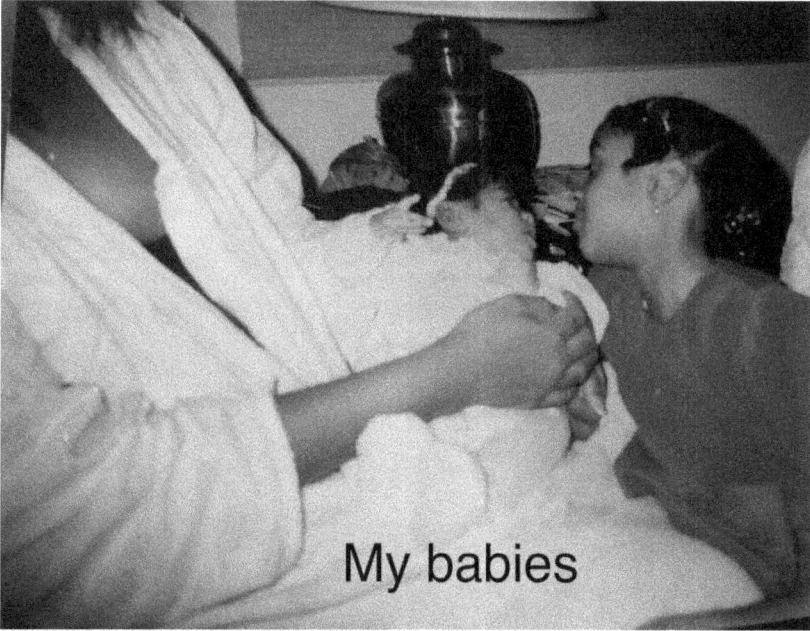

My babies

Family 1999

Masters Degree Recipient

Hubby and Me 2010

40 years old

Easter 2016 my lil guy

Doctors Daughters in effect

My beloved
parents

SELF-ESTEEM

Whenever I hear LeVert's Casanova, I think of two things. The first I think of is my good friend, Sabine, dancing to it at my sweet 16. When we first got the VHS of the party, my mother and I watched it religiously to see Sabine's dance. Even while watching it recently, my younger daughter asked how she made herself move like that. That gal can dance! The second thing I think of is the first guy who really made me question my looks, Steve Lowell. He used to say that his friends said that song was about him, so whenever I heard it back then and even now, I think of him. Before I met Steve, I never really questioned my looks. Growing up I knew I was cute. My mother, in particular, made a big deal that my hair was thick and long for a Black girl. I didn't have waist-length hair like my cousin Mary or my godmother, but it was an abundant amount, and when straightened, it was way past shoulder length. As a little girl, my hair was straightened with a hot comb for special occasions. I wasn't allowed to get a relaxer until I got my first menstrual period (Haitian superstition). Whenever I got my hair straightened, I knew I looked better than when I had the big ole dookie braids.

I recall one year before we went on Christmas vacation at school, we had our annual Christmas party, so we got to dress up, and of course, my hair was pressed and looked really nice. An unexpected (for me) rainstorm came down, and I had no umbrella or hood on my coat, so I ended up having to run in the rain with a half plastic bag that my teacher tried to makeshift as a hat for me as I cried hysterically. When I got on the bus, I continued to cry uncontrollably, and my friends asked why I was so upset. I explained as they tried to tell me that it wasn't a big deal. But that didn't help; as I look back now, I realize I must have looked really stupid. Big crazy-looking hair smelling like a rotten egg (ladies who press and curl...y'all know the deal) with a plastic bag hanging off my head. Man, listen; when I think about it now, I know I was a hot ass mess, but my hair was my thing, and it provided me with a certain comfort that I was pretty. Well, by the time I was 14, I was finally done with the press and curl and was ready for my first relaxer. I remember going into the salon to find out how much it would cost for a relaxer and cut. The minute the word cut was said, the stylist immediately replied, "No, you don't want to cut your hair." You either have two types of hairdressers: the ones who try and tell you not to cut your hair or the scissor-happy ones who want to cut your hair out of jealousy. I met them both. Like I said, having hair as a Black girl (back then) was a rarity, and people either want to cut it off or want to try to preserve it. When I got my hair relaxed and cut into a style, I recall that my mother picked up the hairs that fell on the floor and saved them in a suitcase as a souvenir. Once my hair was done, I had a slightly feathered look and maintained my length. When we left the salon, I was overjoyed and couldn't stop looking in the mirror as my hair was full, long, and bouncy. All the patrons there were looking at me and one lady, which really annoyed me, kept looking at me and laughing even as I left with my mother. I tried not to let it bother me as I walked home with my mother, elated that my hair was done and long gone was the worry about having poofing hair when it got wet. I had that straight nice wet look like the white girls had. I started my freshman year right after getting my hair done and felt ready to welcome a social life involving boys.

Since I went to an all-girls school, we had weekend dances at the boy's school. Knowing I was the shit because of my hair, I thought I'd bag a guy quick fast. Well, things didn't work out as I thought. For one, the pickings were slim. Also, I spent most of the time dancing with my friends. At one of the dances, I saw a familiar character who kept staring at me, and when it finally hit me, I realized he was a former classmate, named Augustus Scott, who went by the name Scottie that went to my elementary school for a moment. He ended up being hugged up on an upperclassman named Shirley, but when everyone did a group dance, he came my way. So, I ended up taking that and running with it, thinking that he was into me. At the time, the group of girls I hung around were really into the "LaSalle" guys and were paired up, so I decided to try and hook up with "Scottie" since he was the only guy I felt I could get at the school. Never mind, he was with Shirley, who was tall, light skin with a mushroom-type cut, but he obviously liked me because I had "long hair." So, I started my campaign to try to get close to him and I really pushed hard to the point that he had a senior in my school approach me and tell me to leave him alone. Talk about egg on your face. I had the whole damn pie.

A classmate and my best friend at school named Perimeter tried to help me get over him by hooking me up with her older brother. I talked to him every night on the phone for about a month when we decided to meet up in person. Once I did meet him, he kept emphasizing how beautiful I was. I was thrilled that a guy was finally telling me this. After that, we kept up with phone conversations, but since he was way older than me; I was 15 and he was 20, he wanted to try getting me alone at his house. At the time it was very hard to maneuver with my parents, so that relationship eventually soured. By the time my school closed, I spent most of my summer going to Queens to stay with my cousins. The allure for me there was the guys that lived across the street and their friends that would hang on the block. My mother would say that these guys were like bees, and we were the honey. Every time we sat on the stoop the guys would flock around. But again, as I quote my beloved mamman we were big, bright (my cousins were very fair skin) healthy girls with long hair so it wasn't a shock. Even though nothing much came out of it, they validated my feelings and gave me a great confidence boost. So, I always looked forward to going there until my cousins moved to Miami, then I was crushed. Not only did I lose my family, but no more guys to flirt with. So, I just tried to focus on school and losing weight, particularly now that I was at my new school which was all white.

Before beginning my junior year, my best friend from elementary school Monique set me up with Steve over the phone. We started talking on a daily basis for about three months, and he seemed real suave. I even remember the code names we had to give him since we weren't supposed to be talking to boys. We called him Sindy, and his friend, Damian Daisy. Steve had a sexy smooth voice and said the right things, but I knew just because his voice was fine didn't mean he was. So, I was in no hurry to meet up with him until he wrote to me and sent me his picture. Back in the day before Instagram, Facebook, Snapchat, camera phones, hell before cell phone period, guys/girls would send pictures via mail. Once he did, I was ready to meet up with him. I still remember what I wore since I had lost a lot of weight and finally had a flat stomach. I wore my acid wash tight jean mini skirt and a Mickey Mouse half shirt. My cousin, Crici, who was spending the weekend with me, was there for moral support. He was supposed to come to my house around five in the afternoon, but he didn't come till nine with some friends, guys and girls. By then, my mother wasn't having it. She answered the door and forbade me to come anywhere near it as she explained that it was too late. When he left driving in front of my house, I opened the door and he saw my shadow. We had some flirty verbatim that I don't recall. The next day when he called, he said, "After I saw that body and all that hair, I will definitely come back to see you." Feeling justified and on cloud nine, I couldn't wait to meet face to face with him. It finally happened a week before school started. Once again, I wore my acid wash mini skirt, black tank top, black high heels, and a matching jacket. We met in front of my house in the early afternoon, and once again, he brought someone with him. He didn't stay that long, and when he left, I asked what he thought. He told me he'd let me know over the phone. Well, I don't recall who called who first, but it was probably me. When we did speak, he severely critiqued my looks. He mentioned that he thought I would have looked like Sheila E. or Apollonia, not some brown skin girl with braces. Did I skip over that part? Well, it's not something I like to talk about, but I had braces from the time I was 10 till I was 16/17. My dentist was a real sadist, but I'll get into that a little later. Any who I allowed what he felt I should look like started to overshadow my thoughts, and to dictate my life. First, I started getting into the whole light skin vs. dark skin scenario. Since I was brown, I felt it didn't apply to me, plus let's not forget my beloved hair put me in a different category. In creole, there is a term for women/girls like me who are brown or darker with long hair known as "beaute creole," translated as creole beauty. Plus, in my opinion, I rather see a darker girl with real hair than a lighter one because it's easily expected for a light skin girl to have long hair, but I digress.

So, I started thinking to myself; if I was lighter, he would have liked me better. To dispute my claim, I asked my male cousin his opinion of light skin girls and dark girls. He told me that lighter skin girls were more attractive to him because they seemed more feminine than darker girls. He also added his two cents by stating my cousin Cricri looked better than me because she was fairer. So, I got an opinion from a guy I wasn't involved with, which solidified the other guy's opinion. Regardless of this, Steve and I still talked on a day-to-day basis, so I felt like things were still good. Plus, when I had a Halloween Party, and I dressed like a sexy devil, he attended. Again, with a friend, who he later told me over the phone gave me the seal of approval. I remember that Monday after I went to school, I felt like everything was going my way. I still had Steve licking at my heels, and I aced an English test at the time. Life was treating me well! This soon changed when I went to get my touch-up. The usual person who did it wasn't there, so I had a new person do it, which wasn't an issue since sometimes I switched up stylists depending on their availability. Anyway, I had this female named Jamie doing my hair, and she said she was just going to just trim it. Instead, she took the scissors to my long locks and proceeded to give me a hideous mullet. Being naive, young, plus I was raised to be a lady and not show out, I didn't say anything. I just started crying as I saw my reflection in the mirror. When my mother picked me up and paid, she was startled. The first thing I did when I got home after staring in the mirror was to take the dirty ice cream dish I had in my room and smash it against the wall as I screamed. My life was totally ruined. Who is going to like me now???? My mother tried to help fix my hair and commented as she put the rollers on that before my hair was too much for the rollers, but now the rollers were too big for my hair. The one good thing about having a Haitian mother is that they know what to do to make your hair grow fast. She immediately started using foltene hair treatment from France at the time, every other night in my hair to help it grow. But my mother, who as you read can see was always brutally honest, would criticize my looks now. She said since I had a big flat nose, I should always have long hair because it softens my look. I spent my whole weekend trying to figure out how I could wear my hair without a hat, and finally settled on using a sweatband to put down the ridiculously short front and put the rest in a ponytail. I went to school and could not stop talking about it. I recall telling some girl named Ryan, and another girl named Marie. Ryan kept laughing, and Marie just stared at me. White girls SMH.

Thank goodness Christmas vacation started right away, and I didn't have to endure my classmates, but my family had made arrangements to go to Miami to visit my cousins. A trip I once looked forward to I now dreaded due to my hair. To make matters worse, I got back my PSAT results the same day we were leaving, and my father had a fit. I got less than a 900, and he went on a tirade of how I was an idiot, I would never get into a good college, and wouldn't be able to make it in life. As far as standardized tests are concerned, I don't believe in them whatsoever. I know colleges base most of their acceptance of students on the SAT or ACT, but these tests cannot measure potential, creativity, and ability. Take me, for instance... My test results would label me a dunce, but how come when I went to Stony Brook for my bachelor's I ended up being on the Dean's List, as well as when I was working on my master's, my first semester I achieved a perfect 4.0. Plus, I graduated with a 3.7 average. Boo-Yah...But getting back to December 1987, pops was furious that coupled with my revolting haircut, I felt like everything was too much. I recall I concocted a plan to make it look like I wanted to kill myself. Growing up watching the after-school specials showing how white parents and families rallied together with their kids, I thought my parents would stop their shouting and yelling and just be nice and comfort me. Dealing with everything I was going through, that's all I wanted. Well, I got the exact opposite when my mother found me lying down with the broken glass from my ice cream dish and the "suicide note." She ran in panic, calling my father who then ran into my room. By this time, I stood up, still crying, and he proceeded to slap me twice. Haitians don't play that soft-ass shit when it comes to that. Well, despite all the dramatics, we did end up going to Miami, and my cousins really tried to help with my hair, but it didn't work. One instance that stood out was an outing to the Galleria Mall. I wore my famed Mickey Mouse crop top and my white short shorts. A group of young guys walked past us, and one guy looked directly in my face saying, "Ugly girl." I was so upset and tried not to let it affect my mood during my vacation, but it did. Once we returned home, I focused on doing everything and anything to make my hair grow out faster. It was during that time I really started thinking about the whole light skin, dark skin thing. I would say to myself if I were lighter with light-colored eyes and European features, particularly my nose, it wouldn't be such a problem. It even translated to me thinking that if I was fairer, I would have been accepted easier in my lily white school. Going to an all-white school was one of the hardest things I ever dealt with as a teen. No matter how much I tried to fit in or tried to be invisible, they always pointed out how different I was. I recall one time a teacher made the mistake of calling someone else my name, and everyone laughed. The girl named Beth asked, "how could you confuse me with Sybil? Because it was so blatantly obvious not to call anyone by my name. I also thought that if I was lighter with waist-length hair and green eyes, maybe it would have been easier to make friends. Since I was not only the one chocolate chip in the cookie, I was also a transfer student, so mostly everybody knew each other. It was harder making friends. I took what I could get, even if it meant making friends with so-called nerds. But don't sleep on nerds, particularly white ones, because they can say some fucked up things too. Like the time I invited my schoolmate Kara to my sweet sixteen, she replied that her father asked if she was going to be the only white person there. Not to mention, when we had to read the classics like *To Kill a Mockingbird* and the word nigger was repeated numerous times, which caused an uneasiness with me in the class. Hell, that probably was the first time the teacher had to endure having an actual Negro in the class. At the end of class, my teacher apologized to me as if it made it any better, and then my friend came and told me how bad she felt for me sitting there and hearing it. I used to think that it would have made the whole thing a lot easier if I wasn't so noticeably "Black".That and dating.

Around that time, music videos were the rage, and every video chick was usually light skin with long hair. *The Cosby Show* and *A Different*

World were on and popping [12]Whitley and Denise, who were portrayed by mixed-race women, were the girls the guys wanted to get with. Hell, to add fuel to the fire, Spike Lee's *School Daze* (one of my favorite movies) had come out that winter, and anyone who saw it remembers the wannabes were light with colored eyes and long hair, while the jigaboos were dark with nappy/short hair. So, for me, the message being sent was that if you're light with long hair, you were right. This obsession continued for over 20 years. As far as Steve was concerned, mentioning Sheila E. set off the obsessive thinking disorder that I now realized I had (have). Turns out during that school year, there was a girl who was the exact replica of Sheila E., and due to my feelings of insecurity, I would develop an unhealthy fixation on this girl, thinking she was dating "my man." Turns out that I discovered she lived in a town near where he was working, so I took that and ran with it. I pictured that they would bump into each other and fall in love leaving me out in the cold. Every day at school, I would look out to see if he would pick her up or eavesdrop on her convo in the girls' room to see if she mentioned him. I even dragged my poor mother and friends at school into this mess. I went on incessantly with this bullshit for the remainder of the year. During that time, Steve became the first guy I ever kissed and allowed him to go to second base. He eventually disappeared in the middle of the year and moved to Florida supposedly. Actually, what happened was that he and Daisy drove down to Florida and ended up getting locked up for stealing sneakers at some mall. "Can I pick um or can I pick um?" I saw him again two years later when I first started college. My hair had finally grown out, my braces removed, and I started to own my looks at 19. Guys were coming to me left and right, so I knew I had this. Like my friend Anna would say, he was "worshiping." I didn't seriously dis him as I should have, but I did let him know I didn't forget what he said to me. He tried to brush it off by saying he wanted to give me an eraser so I could remove everything he said to me from my mind. Go figure. I didn't have any hair issues again until I started seeing hubby. Before I was with hubby, I had let the hair thing get to me a little again.

---

[12] on and popping-hot

After I had given birth to my first daughter, my hair wasn't exactly up to par the way it was before. No one told me age and hormones would affect my once lovely locks. I decided to get an extension/weave added on the back of my hair. I went from shoulder length to almost waist length in three seconds, and I was thrilled. I really thought it would help me attract the right guy, but I still got the same losers. Around 1995, I removed the hair and had a lot of damage to the back. Thank goodness that around that time, the Aniston style was in, so I did a cute bob-ish style for a while, but I took care of my hair like the weave. Still blow-drying and using a curling iron. When I started dating hubby seriously, I started to get serious about my hair. As I stated before, hubby was a very handsome guy, and I would question what he saw in me. Then, I would go over the mental lists of being light versus being dark, especially now as I dated a Haitian guy. Before, the whole light skin/dark skin thing applied only to the guys I was dating, but now it applied to the whole family. Haitians, like most Caribbean people, are very color struck/hair struck. Haitian men, in particular, don't like fake hair whatsoever. Since hubby was from a grand old family that was mostly "high yella[13]" I wanted to show them that I fit in or was his match by getting my hair back in its former glory. I started taking better care of my hair by having it washed and set and looked into anything that would help it grow faster. I even purchased a vibrating hairbrush. SMH. Well, of course, when my hair became my prime focus, I had another setback. I was waiting to relax my hair when my hairdresser at the time told me that she didn't have any more relaxers left. She sent me to the beauty supply to get some more relaxers for her. The guy at the store claimed he didn't have any more left but had this new one made from herbs. Since I wasn't familiar and, in a rush, to get my hair done, I took it. Once I got back to the salon, I got my hair relaxed, and there was no problem. But they used the same relaxer on another client, and her hair started shedding immediately. I kinda got worried, but I kinda pushed back my fear by mentally playing over in my mind that my hair was fine and didn't shed. I left and went about my business until the following

---

[13] high yella-light skinned

week when I came back and saw chunks of hair coming out as they roller-set my hair. I tried not to panic in front of everyone, but anxiety took its root. I went home trying to find my "hair remedies" to fix it and decided right there and then to find a new hairdresser ASAP. And ladies, it was around this time my loving boyfriend went on his "All male vacation" that he promised he wouldn't go on which caused our first fight allowing him to provide me with a halfhearted apology and stating that he was a good-looking guy, he could have anyone he wanted. Talk about perfect timing. I just kept going over and over that which led to brief moments of hysteria. While having these meltdowns here and there, I contacted my cousin Cricri who always had long hair and got a recommendation for a new hairdresser. I started going to her former hairdresser Ella, who got my hair back in tiptop shape, but it wasn't without any controversy. I refused to let her relax my hair after what I went through, and she had to literally coax me like a kid to relax it. I used to hold on to my rosary beads while I got my relaxers thereafter. LOL. It was during those times at Ella's that I shared my fears and insecurities about not being fair skinned. She bossed me up by saying, "So what," and introduced me to the phrase "creole beauty." Once my hair was back up to par, I felt at hubby's level, but I became obsessed with making sure my hair stayed that way. I even went as far as not letting my then five years old go on my bed during the school week for fear of getting lice. I made sure every weekend to check and wash her hair. She never did get it, but years later, she let me know that she had a friend in school who had lice, but she never let me know because she knew I would freak out. I tell you; I was certainly out there when it came to my hair, but when real-life set in with its problems here and there, my hair obsession went out the window.

As far as the light skin vs. dark skin issue and my looks, I think most black women have definitely had issues about being seen as pretty. Growing up as a little Black girl, I know most girls recall putting a towel on their heads pretending that they had long waist-length hair like the little white girls, Spanish girls, Indian girls, and Asian girls. As Black girls, we definitely have it 100x worse having to deal with the European standard of beauty that is thrown at us from left to right. I recall when I read _The Blacker the Berry_ in college. The main character, who was born to a fair skin woman and a dark skin man, came out dark like her father. Her mother would always say that she wished that she was born a boy because it wouldn't have been that bad. I always thought that this was a classic example of how as little girls, we're taught that our looks are everything as opposed to little boys. Even with my daughters, I see the difference in how people will view them. As a mother, I think both are beautiful, but I know some will view my younger one as the prettiest because she is more aesthetically pleasing. She has more European features, is a bit lighter, light eyes, and has long natural hair. Getting older, I have come to realize that even though looks are a big deal, they aren't everything. Looks will not keep a relationship going, looks will not stop anyone from cheating, and looks do not compensate for not doing your part in a relationship, period. That doesn't mean I don't have my days where I criticize myself or feel self-conscious about my breasts, feet, and underbite. I've spent about 10 pages talking about hair; I didn't once mention my underbite. I only just started to notice it about a few years ago. Only big _Star Wars_ franchise fans will understand, but I sometimes feel like my jawline resembles a Gamorrean, one of Jabba's guards. I never really had anyone ever mention it. Oh! Wait, I did. My classmate Annie had a similar underbite. She mentioned out loud in front of all our friends that I should get my jaw wired with hers. Outraged and embarrassed, I yelled no. Also, my daughter's father's friend said my mouth looked like an opened cash register, but I didn't pay him any mind. It wasn't until I caught my image on my wedding video that I tried to pull in my lips if I'm showing my profile. Or if I'm smiling, I make sure not to do any all-out toothy smile because of my rocky shoreline, as my hubby puts it. LOL. Though I love my body, the one thing, well, two things that I would change are my breasts. They are way too small for my body frame. I'm classic pear-shaped, and I would much rather be an hourglass. The only time I ever enjoyed larger breasts was when I was pregnant and nursing. When I was pregnant with my older daughter, they stayed the same throughout the whole nine months, but with my younger daughter, they grew. Ella said that I finally got the right sperm in me ☺. Nursing both my girls, I had full C cups and kinda enjoyed it. The reason was that not only did my breasts get bigger, but my legs, thighs, hips, stomach, and ass did as well. So, I still remained pear-shaped but bigger. Generally speaking, I'm an A-cup and I definitely think a DD would be more appropriate. Now, my feet kinda go hand-in-hand with my breasts. I wear anywhere from a size 8.5 to 10, but usually a size 9, and I'm flat-footed. But I would accept my foot size easier if I had bigger breasts. It's one thing to wear a size 9 shoe but match that with A-cup breasts for me, no bueno. My younger daughter is perfect. She has D-sized breasts and wears a size 7 in shoes. I'm so jealous.

My self-esteem issues have shifted as I've gotten older, from my looks to how I feel about myself. Speaking as someone who suffers from anxiety and depression, I can tell you that how I feel about myself is in correlation with those conditions. Plus, I realized that it doesn't matter how good you look; if you don't feel good inside, it's gonna reflect big time. For me, I know that my anxiety comes from never feeling good enough and a fear of failure. A lot has to do with my upbringing and definitely my time spent in high school. Like I said earlier, being the only Black student in my class really affected me to the point that I noticed I started experiencing my first bout of anxiety during my junior year. I was so scared of doing something to embarrass myself and my race that I ended up developing a "stomach condition" in my head. As I got older, my anxiety reared its head many times and now took form in the fear of failure. Being the only young, unwed single mother in my family/social circle, I felt a lot of pressure to succeed and overcome the stigma that followed me. As my mother used to say, everybody was doing it; having the baby was proof that I had sex, so I was the bad one. Dealing with that label was like walking around branded with the scarlet letter "A." Or in my case, "UW." Family members, particularly my father's sister, would tell my mother that I wouldn't amount to anything. Even my godfather was very skeptical, after having a long talk with him some years after my cult and baby situation, about how I realized I messed up and was ready to make everything right. Single motherhood without a college education and/or marriage, as I stated before, is like the devil with a smile in the Haitian community. When it came time for me to graduate from college, I dealt with the anxiety of believing what was said about me. I started thinking I was gonna fuck up my last year, and I would end up being more of a loser by disappointing my family. I ended up having a full-blown panic attack while I was in class once and immediately had to leave for fear of "wiggin[14]" out in class. It was after that experience that I started much-needed therapy. Fortunately, after getting myself together and through the grace of GOD, I graduated and proved everybody wrong. But as I have stated before, finding work was an absolute nightmare, particularly, after my master's degree. When I did find employment, I let the uneasiness of not finding work get to me. I questioned myself like, what was wrong with me? Why was I unable to find anything? Why wasn't I able to fulfill the goals I set for myself? What if I fuck up and end up in the worst situation? Sad to say that my career and finances have gotten the best of me and have filled me with anger, disappointment, frustration, and at times hopelessness.

As an only child who has lost both parents almost back-to-back, my career/finances have taken more from me than their deaths. Even dealing with my wayward daughter takes a backseat to my financial health and my career endeavors. My girlfriends, those I grew up with, and I try to do a monthly dinner/brunch, but as the offspring of physicians, we call it Doctor's Daughters. We all come together discussing our lives as mothers, wives, ex-wives, fiances, current events, laughing, and relaxing. I can't begin to tell you that even though I have a great time with my sista/friends, I can't help but feel out of place with them. They are either doctors themselves, lawyers, nurses, directors, managers, etc., making six figures if not close to that amount a year while I work as a non-exempt telephone representative making an hourly wage not too far from the minimum wage. Honestly speaking, I feel that way mostly around lots of folks that I don't measure up professionally. Now, I know as long as I don't beg, borrow, or steal from anyone and I maintain myself it shouldn't matter; but to ME, it does. I

---

[14] wiggin out-losing it mentally

could understand my vocational outcome if I only had a high school diploma, but as a three time college graduate, it's a heavy blow to deal with, and it looms over me, so to speak. It's so apparent that someone even mentioned it at my gym that they see a sense of sadness in my eyes. For the past 40 odd years, I've been taught to believe in cause and effect. Being raised as a Roman Catholic, you were taught from the pulpit to the nuns in school that whatever happened, you did something to deserve it. For every situation occurring, this is the one that I can't seem to fathom, and I continue to ask myself why. Like I mentioned earlier, my parents dying within a short time span of themselves is something that is still heartbreaking as well, but that's GOD'S doing, not mine. I had no control over their life expectancy, so there's really nothing I can do regarding that except to grieve and move on. As is with my daughter's "lifestyle". I have no control. But my career is supposed to be something I have control over. If I'm not happy where it is or where it's going, I should be able to get up and leave, right? I mean, isn't that what these so-called gurus tell you if you're not happy to make the necessary changes. Particularly, when it comes to employment, they usually advise that if you're not satisfied with your line of work, get up and walk away. Well, how do you walk away when this is the main source of your livelihood???? So, basically, I feel trapped. Aside from my feelings of entrapment, I'm fucking furious, overwhelmed, saddened, and most of all disappointed. Disappointed that apart from everything else going on in my life, I'm also dealing with this, which is a major weight.

I mentioned GOD earlier, and I can say in good conscience that I am angry at HIM to a certain extent. Any holier than thou Christian type reading this must be hitting the brakes quick fast like wait, what? Well, I'm not going to sugarcoat my feelings because I'm talking about GOD. I'm not one of these Jesus freaks[15] that think every little thing is a sin and the enemy is at large. I was made in the image of GOD, and that includes my emotions. Plus, GOD is bigger than everything, then HE can handle my being mad at HIM. Getting older, I have realized that all

---

[15] Jesus freaks-overzealous Christians

these silly rules about not being mad at GOD and blasphemy are bullshit. If I truly have a relationship with GOD like I have with anyone, it must be truthful. Also, as with any relationship, there will be ups and downs. Now, I've done many prayers, fasting, and even tried tithing in order to get my career/financial life to no avail. My cousin Jeannie, who is a devoted Seventh Day Adventist, says that if I converted, this part of my life would change for the better. Even my close friend Melinda, at one of my worst times, questioned me by stating, "Don't you pray?" And I recall speaking to a nun at my church once when I wanted to get answers as to why GOD was letting this happen to me. She responded that GOD gave us free will, so in essence, she was saying this was my fault that I was in my current predicament. Well, I know for a fact that I didn't purposely set out to be here, as far as my cousin is concerned I told her there was no need to convert because I worship the same GOD, and as far as my prayerful devotion is concerned, it shouldn't be questioned. I finally realized bad things happened that turn people's world upside down, and no matter how much you pray, sometimes the answer isn't what you expected or when you expect it. You know you keep hearing that if you do certain things i.e., thankfulness, tithing, and fasting GOD will bless you well, I'm here to tell you I don't think that's the case. GOD is not a magician. There's no magic word or thing to do to get HIM to work. No matter how soon we need that certain thing, GOD is gonna go according to HIS time and no one else's. I'm not saying stop praying, and I'm not trying to promote positive thinking since I sure as hell don't follow it to a T, but I'm saying that maybe it's a matter of making it through the eye of the storm. Like Edmond Dantes from one of my favorite movies, *The Count of Monte Cristo* 2002 version said, "Life is a storm, my young friend. You will bask in the sunlight one moment and be shattered on the rocks the next. What makes you a man is what you do when that storm comes." Well, I'm walking in the storm with my raincoat, hat, and umbrella, steadily walking to get to the other side.

TALKING/ACTING WHITE WHILE BEING BLACK

I'm going to bring up a subject that every middle to upper-class Black person has dealt with more than once in their life. Behaving/talking like you're white. I'm not sure if, in other cultures, it's such a big deal as it is in the Black world, but it's often seen as one of the biggest betrayals. As a member of the first generation of Haitian Americans, we are often at the brunt of our African American brothers and sisters due to our mannerisms and speech. Growing up, our parents made sure to educate us, so we do not turn out to be the cookie-cutter, stereotypical Black person. I don't know if it has to do with trying to emulate the French culture that so influenced our people, but we were taught early on that our speech and demeanor would make us stand out for the best and provide us better opportunities. My godbrother once shared with me a story about him having dinner with his friend's family. He grew up upstate in a white populated area and was invited to have dinner at his white friend's house for the first time. After dinner was complete, he said his friend's mother told him, "I'm so glad you're not like one of them." Back then, as he explained it to me, he (we) took it as a compliment, but now as we know better (well, I know better; I'm not throwing shade[16] , just not sure if he agrees) and realize that was just as racist a statement as ever. But as I look back, I guess our families were trying to teach us that with our behavior and communication, we could elevate our race and not be hindered by it.

My elementary school, Sacred Heart Seminary, was in Hempstead in the heart of a neighborhood filled with Blacks, Whites, and Latinos. My best friend at the time, Monique, kept me current with Black culture on a day-to-day basis. I still recall the first two rap songs I learned were from her. We were always in the classroom rapping '*F-R-E-S-H Fresh Fresh yo that grea*t,' or '*It might sound sad it might sound funny, but that's what people Do For Money*'. Every weekend we watched *New*

---

[16] shade-underhanded insult

114

York Hot Tracks and would discuss the songs and videos we saw Monday morning. I continued to keep up to date with the trends at my high school in Amityville, which was mostly Black. At the time, the school was located in the heart of a bad neighborhood, and I made friends with a mixture of girls, but mostly Black. When my school closed down, I was sent to Our Lady of Mercy Academy in Syosset. Syosset was and still is an area mostly populated by affluent whites. I entered in the fall of 1986 as a sophomore and the lone Black student in my class. Back then, Black culture wasn't considered hip and trendy. Diddy didn't bring rap and hip hop to the masses, yet and White America wasn't appropriating it at the time, so hip-hop culture was just beginning to flourish. I wasn't allowed to listen to rap. My father hated rap music and he associated it with hoodrat[17] mentality. He thought it brought out the worst in Black people and thought it was going nowhere. Little did he know it would be a billion-dollar industry providing an opportunity for many. Back then, my everyday interactions were with a bunch of Beckies,[18] so little by little, I began to absorb their culture. Since I wasn't allowed to listen to rap, I listened to top 40. Z100 and 95.5WPLJ were my go-to stations. *NY Hot Tracks* was slowly replaced by *Dance Party USA*. I remember talking to a friend on the phone who went to a Catholic High school in a mixed area, and I said something about a girl in my class by stating that she was so funny; I said she was a "pisser." She was taken aback and told me not to ever say that again. But I continued to get deeper and deeper in my assimilation. Not only was I speaking proper English, but I did start to have the sing-songy tone of a carefree white girl, and I used "like" in every other word when I spoke. Even after I graduated from high school, it still stuck with me. I recall when I first started dating my daughter's father, he got really upset about my enunciation of his name. Not only was my way of speech and mannerism affected, but my style of dress as well. In the 80s, there were two types of styles for white girls. There was the preppy deppy JAP style with polo, khakis, and baggy jeans, or the Guidette look with the big

---

[17] hoodrat-no or low class
[18] Beckies-white girls

hair, bright colors, and tight clothes. Since I love anything form-fitting, I gravitated towards the guidette look. When I was bigger, I wore a lot of leggings and big tops. I hardly ever wore any jeans, but when I lost the weight, I showed off my figure. One summer as I worked in the mall, I wore a tight pair of acid wash jeans, a big gaudy belt around my hips, a white with black polka dots slightly cropped top; meaning you couldn't see my stomach unless I moved around, white thick slouchy socks, and a pair of white slip-on keds and my hair styled like Pebbles Flintstone as a teen. A guy and his friend tried to talk to me. Like any girl who's not interested, I ignored them. As the guy walked away, he said out loud, "Never mind you too white for me."

Back then, Black girls didn't dress feminine and girly as they do now. Black girls, or should I say hood girls, dressed like a more or less feminine version of the guys with baggy jeans or baggy pants, Adidas track suits, baggy tops, and eventually the bamboo earrings. Since none of that appealed to me and I was all about advertising what I had, I showed it off. Growing up, I was a big girl and got made fun of by Black and white kids, but that stopped as I hit my teen years, maybe because I got taller, but my weight kinda even out with my height a little. When I was 15, I must have been 5'6, 150lbs, size 13/14, and a little overweight but not outwardly noticeable. In the middle of my sophomore year, I decided to get in shape and started my own exercise and regime plan. At first, my goal was to be able to wear the fashionable clothes that I loved, but then I wanted to emulate the thin, lithe bodies of the white girls that were around me. My goal weight was to be 125lbs and a size 7, and within a couple of months, I ended up meeting that goal. I got a lot of compliments about how good I was looking. But I ended up taking it too far once I reached my goal weight and decided I needed to be 115 lbs. Nowadays, for me, it's all about being shapely, and if someone calls me thin, I get highly offended, but back then, I would have been so happy I'd be doing backflips. I wanted to be really skinny, particularly my legs. I have and am now proud of my big shapely ham hock legs, which I got from my papa, but back then, I hated them. Since I'm pear-shaped, when I lose weight, the first thing that goes are my arms, chest, and stomach.

It takes my hips, thighs, butt, and legs a good minute to catch up. Well, I wanted to have long, straight stick legs like some of the white girls had. I wanted to be flat and straight with no curves except for boobs. When I wasn't reaching my goal weight fast enough, I took the advice of a girl at school. That's one thing for sure; white girls know what to do when it comes to losing weight fast. She said she lost 15lbs in a week by eating one thing a day. So, I did that plus exercised and met my target, but in the process, I ended up fucking up my stomach something awful. It wasn't till I started hanging with my short and shapely Puerto Rican friend, Anna, that my body image changed. She would always say that guys, particularly Black ones, would come up to her and say that she had a nice butt. She also got on me about being too thin. She was the one that taught me that if I wear leggings, it should never be hanging off my butt. No bagginess whatsoever. So, thanks to Anna's severe criticism, my stomach problem, and everything else. I started to eat like a normal person and got my body to a curvy pear shape.

Body image wasn't the only area affected by white folks. It even impacted how white people perceived me as a Black person as well. One time I was hanging out with my friend Monique, and I needed to use the payphone. There was a white girl jawing[19] away on it. I went and stood there for about three minutes, and she continued to keep on talking. I went back to my car and told Monique it was gonna be a while. Monique said, "Let me show you how it's done." She got out of the car and stood right where I stood with her arms and face crossed; the girl hung up almost immediately. Monique at 5 '0 with her geometrical haircut, bamboo earrings, long and excessively decorated nails, and leather African medallion symbol between her massive breasts, was not to be messed with. When she got back in the car, I asked her how she did that and she said she looked intimidating while I looked like one of them happy go lucky. I was branded an OREO, Black on the outside and white on the inside. Among my family friends, no one singled me out (well, depending on where they lived, I had two cousins, one residing in Merrick Queens, and one in Rosedale who said I talked like a white girl)

---

[19] jawing-talking

because we all spoke the same way, but whenever I was around other Blacks the first thing that was brought up was my speech. In the summer of 1988, I spent one week at my godmother's house in Scarsdale with her kids. We went clothes shopping at the Galleria Mall, and while Sabine, the oldest and responsible one, was shopping for and with her younger brother, Martine, the younger sister, and I caught the attention of a group of guys. We ran up and down the mall trying to avoid them, but at the same time, enjoying the chase. GOD, I miss being young. We finally let them catch up to us and started talking with them, the first thing that came out of their mouths was, "Why y'all talk like that?. Like y'all white." Martine tried to explain and let them know we spoke like this because we were educated, but they weren't trying to hear it. Once I started to date my daughter's father and hang around more of his friends, I started to emulate their way of speech as well. Particularly, after an incident at the train station when a young white woman came out of nowhere and cursed me out. I got out of the car and went inside to confront her; since I wasn't alone, my friends went with me as I cursed her out the white girl style with the accent and everything. One friend just kept laughing at me once we got back in the car, and the other eventually let me know I dead ass sounded like a white chick. Growing up as a young person, you want to fit in so badly with your environment that you try to imitate it as much as possible. As a Black girl in an all-white school, I already stood out due to my color, but my speech didn't have to be an issue particularly since I already spoke correctly; it was a snap to just copy what I heard around me. Plus, my parents made a point to remind me as the only Black student within my class that I needed to not do anything to make me stand out, and so I had to try and stay under the radar; even if it meant compromising my Blackness. As I write this I think of my dancing 😂OH LORDT. My sweet sixteen party is on VHS and is a direct proof of my dancing like a white girl. Nowadays, every girl, regardless of race does the booty pop[20] , so there is really no such thing to me anyway, but back then, I burned up the dance floor like a white chick. My dancing has never really been on point when it comes

---

[20] booty pop-shaking your ass or twerking

to hip hop, but throw on some Haitian music and I will put anyone to shame (thank you, papa).

Once I left that atmosphere and found myself surrounded by people who looked like me, I started to absorb the hip hop culture that was around me. However, my parents were upset because I was becoming like "*vye blackyo*" meaning those bad Blacks. Now, before I get my black card revoked[21] Let me explain. Some of you may know, but for those who don't know, pay attention. Haiti was the FIRST and ONLY free Black republic in 1804 as a result of a successful slave rebellion which took place over 13 years. We, as Black slaves, acquired OUR independence way before the freedom-loving USA whites freed their Black slaves, so we basically gave the Europeans and Americans a big F-you sign which, of course, didn't sit well with either party. So, knowing we defeated these large parties and the system, most if not every Haitian has a certain arrogance, especially if you are educated. Despite what is always seen on TV about Haiti and that we are the poorest nation in the Western Hemisphere, which is a systemic punishment from the whites for the audacity of Blacks gaining their freedom, we do have a variety of social classes among our people. Most Haitians, like my parents, love all things having to do with education, culture, and etiquette. My father was upper-middle-class and my mother middle class, so even though they didn't grow up rich, they had the wealthy mentality when it comes to manners, comportment, and speech. They see it as a way of respect, elevating ourselves, and expanding our opportunities, particularly in Haiti. It also demonstrates having ambitions and wanting something better for ourselves. Bad behavior is viewed as being loud, belligerent, and ignorant. When my parents saw me adapting to what I deemed African American culture, they were disappointed and shocked because I wasn't raised to act like that. As I changed my speech, my clothing as well came into effect. Now, this was pre-Islam, so I was dressing like a typical hood chick. Gone were the pastel colors, tight pants, and big hair. I now embraced the baggy jeans, dark colors, hoodies, and sneakers look. Now, anyone who knows me now knows I'm all about the high heels

---

[21] black card revoked-a Black person making Black people look bad

and usually wear sneakers only to the gym. I brought my last pair of sneakers back in 2010 and recently upgraded because the old ones were falling apart, so as I look back now, to see myself wearing sneakers on a regular basis is totally foreign. But at the time, I allowed my environment to dictate my look. I was so proud of my transformation, and since I was finally embracing what I felt was Black culture I felt I had to show it off particularly to the whites who helped make me who I was. So, under the guise of going to get my transcripts from high school, I drove my father's luxury Volvo blasting Public Enemy dressed in baggy black jeans, an oversized t-shirt, and a black and red Starter Chicago Bulls hooded jacket completed the outfit. My hair was slicked back into a bun with the door knocker earrings. I walked into the building with an air of confidence and arrogance. I knew who I was, and they couldn't take it from me if they tried.

In addition to my transformation, I acquired bad conduct as well. My parents used to take me to this Mexican restaurant called Don Juan's, which was my favorite place to eat. When I was around 19 and Hakeem went on tour, I tried going there with "my friends" once, and shall I say it was an experience. I drove everyone there hoping to have what I now enjoy as a girls' night out, but not with this group. The waiter was polite and tried to take our order, but the girls I went out with weren't used to this and were so defensive and hostile. I wasn't used to this, and I tried to be nice but felt like I was being judged and sentenced by my peers, so I even tried to be like them and acted rudely. But the one thing I would never do is cross the line and steal. When I was five years old, I stole a Tinkerbell nail polish and lipstick set from A&S while shopping with my parents one night. At the store, I asked them to purchase it for me and they said no, so I literally took matters into my own hands and snatched it. When I got home, my mother saw the evidence and told my father who gave me a beating I would never forget. Many years later, I was discussing the incident with my mother, and she said my father did that to make sure I never stole anything again. Well, apparently, it worked because that night, as we left the restaurant, the girls individually started showing off how they stole napkins, knives, forks, and a highball glass off the table.

Once my relationship was over and I returned home after my unfortunate experience, I also returned to my roots and being me. Now, some people say that college-minded Blacks usually don't have a problem with other Blacks speaking properly, but I beg to differ. When I went back to school, I made two new Black friends who almost immediately pointed out my speaking voice, but then again, they weren't exactly from the Upper East Side, so I guess it makes sense. One time I had a collection agency call me (Hey, we've all been there once or twice) regarding a medical bill, while the representative was going over the terms after confirming my name, she asked if I was friends with someone named Sheree and I told her yes, we started talking a little about Sheree and then she told me she wasn't sure whether or not to ask me since I sounded white. SMH. Even dating, my potential suitors would say something about the way I acted. From 1990 to 2000, *Beverly Hills 90210* was the rage for me, well actually until 1997; but anyway, I had a wicked crush on Luke Perry's character, Dylan McKay. When I first started dating darling hubby, he told me he had a Porsche, and the first thing that came out of my mouth was, "Oh my God, you're like Dylan." As soon as I said that, he replied, I knew you were like one of those wanna be white girls watching *90210*. When I mentioned the exchange to a white girlfriend at the time, she laughed and even added that she couldn't believe I said that. My own children who have grown up in a predominantly white neighborhood also feel mommy isn't Black enough. I guess nowadays, with Black/hip hop culture being more rampant and socially acceptable than in my time, my kids view mommy as wanting to be white. My youngest was listening to a popular rap song the other day. She asked me if I liked it. I replied I didn't, and she said to me, "Mommy, you're barely Black" 😊. Even her white friend chimed in by agreeing with her by stating I'm one of those wanna be white Blacks.

The one place my conduct and speech worked in my favor was at work. The first real job I got at a **CALL CENTER** I was originally hired during the holiday season as a temp, but the manager approached me and hired me permanently, noting I communicated very well on the phone. Customer service positions almost always require that you have pleasant telephone manners. Meaning you speak in a clear and audible fashion to your customer in a respectful way. No use of slang, and or jargon providing the information in a concise and succinct manner. Recently, my supervisor heard me on the phone speaking with a patient and commented on how well I spoke. I know if my mother was alive, she would have stated, well, what do you expect from someone who is educated? In a way, it's that, but I also know when and where to use my "white voice." Like Dave Chappelle said, every Black person is bilingual; we know when to use our office voice and when to use our street voice. This brings me to my position scheduling appointments at Family Planning. I can't help but be shocked and amazed as to how some people call their doctor's office. I have been hit with slang, cursing, defensive attitudes, and outright rudeness when trying to acquire necessary information. I know that not everyone was raised alike; but for me, when calling a physician's office, particularly the doctor that examines your WHO HA[22] I think you need to provide respect for the people that work there and most importantly for yourself. This isn't your friend's house around the corner, or the beauty parlor up the street. This is a healthcare facility that provides GYNECOLOGICAL services, so you cannot call there as if you're calling your cable or cell phone company regarding your service. That's why a lot of us get reprimanded because we give it right back to them. Now, we don't curse back (we could never do that without getting fired), but we let them know that we will not tolerate their rude ass behavior. Then, we all discussed how we couldn't comprehend how some people have the nerve to contact a doctor's office like that, which our supervisor kept reminding us that not everyone is raised alike. Etiquette, etiquette, etiquette, and common sense are what goes screaming through my head.

Being raised with manners and decorum, I used to think only applied to the educated middle to high-class Haitians, but I now realize that's not

---

[22] WHO HA-vaginia

the case. It wasn't until fairly recently that I started to recognize that Haitians did not own the right to being well educated, good behavior, and appropriateness. In fact, there was a time, especially after my unfortunate "religious experience," and time spent with my daughter's father and his friends, that I basically held my nose up and snubbed most Black Americans. I started to apply my parents' way of thinking to a level 10 and thought that things would be much better for me if I avoided certain people and made friends with more Huxtable type folks. I remember one time I was walking to the bank and some guys started to "cattle call" me; I tried not to pay attention and continued to move on, but something in me told me to respond back, and I told them, ".....I'm better than you cause I'm Haitian." Well, you should have seen my face when they responded back to me in creole. That's right, they were Haitian, and they proceeded to cuss me out in my own language. I ended up catching a swarm of flies with my mouth so wide open. At the time, I had just graduated from college, and I felt like I had risen from the stereotypical uneducated Black single mother label. Plus, while in college, I minored in Africana Studies, where learning about Haiti and the only successful slave rebellion in history was a big portion in most of the classes I took. I became proud to embrace my Haitian roots that I once shunned. In a way, I justified my actions as making up for all those years ago when I tried to be something I wasn't, which was unrefined, unpolished, and ignorant. It even got to a point once when I was discussing with my friend, other Monique, about a musical artist who was working with a rap/hip hop artist, and I was like how she could lower herself and be around that genre. Other Monique who is Haitian as well called me out and said I sounded like my parents. Like I said earlier, my parents hated rap and they grew to dislike it even more after my experience with my rapper boyfriend left me a "typical baby mama." So, their revulsion towards rap/hip hop was implemented by yours truly for a time. I think what also further influenced my behavior was that I felt that all the good things (doing better in school/graduating college, met, dated, and now engaged to would-be hubby, and a better relationship with my family) were due to my change. But experience like the one I mentioned before and more started to open my eyes.

Growing up and being raised as a "bougie,[23]" you're not really taught how to defend yourself. More emphasis is placed on being well-mannered. Add that with a Catholic education for 12 years where you are always taught to turn the other cheek and you have a dangerous combination. I'll always remember when I was 17, and I had an emergency involving my mother and having to call my papa at the hospital. Since I was freaking out and unable to get in touch with him, I called the nurse or receptionist in his department a bitch. Once everything was resolved, my father understandably made me apologize to his co-worker. One thing that stuck out from that experience was hearing my father on the phone with her saying, "....yes, she is a very nice girl," so I made sure I stayed a "nice girl" no matter what. You usually hear about how ghetto/ hood kids grew up playing the dozens to keep them on their toes so other kids wouldn't mess with them. I remember all of us doctors's kids would watch shows like *What's Happening, Good Times, and The Jefferson* to learn about how to fight back verbally. In seventh grade, John Carao called me all types of the word *fat* to my face, so I decided to take it a step further and call him a "Honky" which I heard from those shows. I thought it would stop him from additional verbal torture, but he then threatened to report me to our school principal. As someone who was never in any real trouble, I started to panic. But thankfully, my friends were able to talk him out of it. After that experience, I made sure I never tried that again. But growing up, you learn that trouble sometimes comes looking for you, and what other choice do you have but to stand up for yourself. During my junior year, I had an issue with two seniors. One time during lunch, my friends and I were talking, and this tall, portly blonde girl walked into the cafeteria as we snickered. She, in turn, told her bosomy friend who approached us and we denied it. But that wasn't enough for the heavyset chick who continued to give us death stares and screamed at the top of her lungs. "You better stop talking about me!" Well thinking that was the end of it, I went on with my life, but she started a campaign against me with her busty friend, who incidentally looked like

---

[23] bougie-bourgeois

Apollonia, who if you recall from my previous chapter, was one of the girls I mentioned that I wished I looked like. Any who, they basically started giving me a hard time, and I tried not to get any negative notice in this lily-white school and tried to ignore it. But it got back to the Dean of Students, Sr. Katherine, who called me in the office to find out what was going on since it was brought to her attention. She stated that they were harassing me because I was black, and I burst out into tears. Trying to be a good Black who didn't make trouble was wearing on me. Once she comforted me, she assured me that I wouldn't have any more problems from the girls, then I left her office. When I got home, I called my friend, Monique, who still went to a mixed school and remained up to date when it came to urban current events. She let me know that under no circumstance was I supposed to accept "that shit" from those white girls. I don't remember word for word what she said, but I recall she spoke distinctly with an urban flair. She let me know that I had to use my Blackness to my advantage and get ghetto[24] with these girls. Well, thanks to Sr. Katherine, I never had any more problems from them, but thanks also to Monique as I was ready if the shit went down. Though those girls never bothered me again, other enemies surfaced, and this time I used my Blackness to my advantage. One time, Lizette Anconi, who was the class goof off and sort of troublemaker, tried to come for me[25] because I hung around a bunch of nerds. The nerds were scared of her and she probably thought that I would be as well, so she said something stupid, and I mumbled under my breath, trying to ignore it. But she kept at it by saying "excuse me" in an accusatory tone which prompted me to let out my rage in the form of "SUCK MY NIGGA ASS BITCH" and walked away. I felt victorious, vindicated, and validated. That line would eventually be my go-to phrase when I got really pissed. During my senior year, I tried the swirl[26] with a guy from our brother's school. I recall sharing my apprehension with a teacher about getting involved with my first interracial hook-up. She warned me to be careful since most white guys viewed Black girls as just a good time and nothing

---

[24] ghetto-rough, hard
[25] come for me-to start with me
[26] swirl-dating a white guy

125

more. Well, it turns out that she was right. We; the dude and I, were at a graduation party together, and he tried to go further than I was ready to go while we were kissing. I told him no, and he basically lost his shit. He pounded his fist against my car, started screaming, and angrily walked away. I really don't recall what happened next, but I do remember going back to the party to get my friends, and standing on the staircase before leaving, telling him, "SUCK MY NIGGA ASS YOU WHITE ASS HONKY" and walking away. Mind you, I was in a room of white folks, and the friends I left with were white as well.

The time spent at that school trying to be one of them as a passive good little Negroes was not working in my favor. I started to realize that I had to stand up for myself. Well, little by little, I grew myself a pair and stood my ground in school, especially when it came to white people, but when it was Black people, it was a whole different ball game. I really wouldn't say anything and tried to let it go. Like I remember one time, me and my friend, Anna were waiting for the bus when a group of Black guys came by and tried to accost us. Well, one of the guys got too fresh, and he squeezed my ass. I yelled something like, 'how dare you?' A group of girls on the bus who were Black happened to be watching and one of them said out loud as we got on, "she's so stupid, I would have slapped him in the face." I remember telling my friend, Anna, to be cool and not react to them. Anna even told me that I didn't have to show that I was so scared. It was then I knew that the reason I never pushed the incident further was that I was indeed scared. Scared that I wasn't Black enough, thereby, I wouldn't be able to defend myself properly. Plus, most Black girls I know had a way of cutting you down to size with their verbatim that would leave you speechless, and I wasn't about to be a victim. Well, it wasn't until recently that I let that type of thinking go and started to fight back regardless. One time, during the many moments of my unemployment, I went to my local library to use the internet, and a stereotypical Black chick with pink extensions, pregnant, and all was sitting next to me. I could tell she was gonna be a problem, so I tried to keep to myself, but this one was looking for trouble. She had something to say about everything to her apparently silent, long-suffering boyfriend. I started laughing about some email; as I looked at the corner of my eye, I saw her staring me down. So, I decided I wanted to be a bitch and started breathing heavily. She turned to me and told me I needed to stop breathing so hard. That was all I needed to let loose, and we got into a heated verbal altercation that resulted in all three of us getting thrown out of the library. I know the argument didn't have to go that route, but she represented all those quarrels and run-ins that I didn't engage in when I was a teen and even as a young adult because I felt inadequate in my Blackness.

Getting older now, I realize my Blackness is not determined by my speech, the way I dress, the music I like, the food I eat, the books I read, the men I like, and the friends I have. My Blackness is determined by my physicality and my experiences. And if I may quote former President Obama, "There is no authentic way to be Black."

PAPA

'I'm not ashamed to say that no man I ever met was my father's equal, and

I never loved any other man as much." Hedy Lamar.

I'll never forget when I knew my papa was going to die. While he was in the hospital in a coma, I dreamed that my father, my mother, and I were all in a car with papa driving. My mother was in front next to him, and me in the backseat like the good old days. Well, as he was driving, he passed out, and I proceeded to climb into the front seat and started driving. Leaving just my mother and me. My father eventually passed away very soon after that dream, and life was never the same.

My father was born, Francois Marie Thebaud, on May 12, 1940, in Gonaives, Haiti, to a prominent lawyer and his wife. My father was the second of their four children, and from what I was told, the brightest. My mother would say that you could tell my father was very intelligent due to his large ears. I recently found his old report cards, and even though they are in French, the results still translate as A+. My father was extremely clever and loved learning. So, you can imagine why having a child that was a B-/C student who wasn't interested in school didn't sit well with him. As I mentioned earlier, when I told him I wanted to be a fashion designer, he told me I could not pursue it because it was not an intellectual career. My father was an academic through and through and wanted me to be a doctor like him. My papa left his beloved country of Haiti to continue his training as a medical doctor and pursue a better life by coming to New York. He got himself settled first before returning for his wife, my mother. My father did his residency at Queens Hospital Center and lived at a family friend's house for four years. My birth and arrival prompted him to get a home of his own. So, we moved to Hempstead, New York, before my first birthday. In fact, the first celebration they had was my first birthday party. From the time I was one until I was sixteen, my papa always made sure to celebrate my birthday in style. He always made a big deal out of our birthdays. It was a week or two before my mother's birthday, so he would come up to me when I was little and be like, it's your mummy's birthday. What are we going to get her? He always involved me in the planning. Papa was a selfless man when it came to gift-giving and went out of his way to make sure we were happy with our gifts. One Christmas, he had my mother open her gift, and she saw a man's shoebox. Amused, she continued to open the box to find a smaller box with a diamond ring. As for myself, I had every Barbie and Barbie product in the Western world until I was around 11. On my 10th birthday, my papa gave me a 10-speed bike that I woke up to find in my room in the middle of the night. My first reaction was that we were being robbed, and the burglar stationed his bike in my room. SMH. Through the years, I managed to rack up quite a lot. As an only child, there wasn't anything that I wanted that I couldn't have. The gifts also didn't stop at just my mother and me; he was very generous with his friend's kids as well. I recall every Christmas Eve, we would go and deliver gifts to my cousins, godbrother/godsister, and friends. As an adult, the Christmases we've had only provided gifts for other kids if we were invited to someone's home for the holidays and vice versa.

Since Catholic school is the prerequisite of almost every Haitian kid, my parents sent me to Sacred Heart Seminary for my elementary education. It was assumed that I would go on to their high school, but since my grades weren't up to par, I didn't get in and ended up having to go to a different Catholic high school. Speaking of grades, as I mentioned before, school wasn't my strong suit at the time, and I got into a lot of trouble because of my grades. Papa would try and work with me doing homework, but it would end up a crying jag for me because he was so strict and would hit me if I gave the wrong answer. Papa wasn't abusive, but he came from a background and time when physical discipline was the norm. He would yell and sometimes curse. Well, not really cursing, just kept saying "goddammit," but with his booming voice, it was quite scary to a little kid/eventual teen. My papa was 6'2, and around 250lbs, as he got older, a lot of people said he resembled and sounded like James

Earl Jones. He was quite intimidating. Even though my mother would lose her temper and discipline me, it wouldn't be the same as my papa punishing me. When I got out of line, the belt or his hand came flying. "Wait till your father gets home" was a very scary prospect growing up. Especially when I knew I did something bad. That's why when I started to get into my boy crazy phase, I made sure not to let anyone see or meet him. My father could be quite rude, especially to strangers and those he deemed that he was better than. Let's face it, the guys I was into were not exactly clean-cut and wholesome. When I say better, I flat out have to say arrogant but not in a harmful way. You see, my father's arrogance came from his love for his country and being a proud Haitian. His nationalism toward his beloved country extended to his way of thinking and the way he raised me. From the time I was two, he sat me on his knee and taught me how to speak Haitian Creole. His theory behind that was not only that I was bilingual, but when I went to Haiti on vacation, he wanted me to fully understand everyone. Where French is considered the proper language of the elite and well educated in Haiti, creole is more of a slang and used when you are familiar with someone. It's usually the language you use when you are "speaking to the help." Also, creole is usually spoken amongst adults while the children are expected to speak French. By the time I was four, I was fluent in French and creole. At one point, I went shopping with papa and my uncle *Ton Ton Bob*. While we were being helped by two females, my uncle started talking about the women saying one of them had a nice ass. He said it in creole, thinking I wouldn't understand. His face dropped as I responded to him in creole, asking which one of them. Papa roared with laughter due to *Ton Ton Bob's* shock that a little kid understood and answered him. My papa also instilled my love of Haitian music and taught me how to dance to it. Whenever we were at a party, he made sure to give me a twirl on the dance floor. One Christmas vacation in Florida, we took over the dance floor and impressed everybody there. Everyone was so surprised to see that I dance compa so well. When they asked my mother, she told them my father taught me since I was a little girl.

In 2005, I went to Las Vegas for my birthday and for the first time. I ended up winning $1200 in blackjack. Papa taught me how to play when I was around eight years old. He came back from a medical conference in Vegas, and I recall he brought me the mini deck of cards as a souvenir. The first thing he did was teach me how to play 21. He also introduced me to my love of swimming. From the time I was a little girl, he got me a mini blow-up pool. Whenever we went on vacation, the first thing we did was swim together. Since he saw I loved the water so much, he enrolled me at the local YMCA for swimming lessons from the time I was six. Unfortunately, since I spent most of my adult life relaxing my hair, I avoided pools like the plague for fear of damaging my precious locks. It wasn't until fairly recently I started swimming again and stunned my darling hubby on our Florida vacay. He ended up sharing with papa how shocked he was that I was such a good swimmer. With a prideful look, papa told him, oh yeah, she definitely knows how to swim very well.

When men take on the role of husband and father, they are supposed to provide for their families. Even though times have changed, I truly believe that a man's role, regardless of if his wife is working, should go above and beyond to maintain his family financially. Well, my father, despite being a medical doctor, held down three jobs as a physician. Each job provided a source of income for a different aspect of our lives. He was an excellent provider, and we never wanted anything. One job he held was solely to pay for my college education. Due to the fact he worked many jobs, he was never home. So, once I hit my teen years, was driving, and involved with boys, I was able to get away with a lot. When I got involved with my daughter's father and his friends, I just flat out stopped going to school. My father wasn't thrilled, but despite his disappointment, he tried coaxing me into getting back to school by trying to upgrade my used car to a newer one. Now, when I look back at that, I realize and know I didn't deserve a new car, but he was really trying to do what he could to make me get on the right track. Fortunately, I didn't get the new car. Knowing me back then, I would have just used it to take "my friends" out and nothing more. When my screwing up was becoming fully evident and no sight of change anytime soon, my papa tried the strict approach, which resulted in all of us getting into an all-out argument. At one point, I think I was getting loud, and he lost his temper and tried to choke me. My mother, of course, intervened and stopped him before it went too far. At the time, I was so upset, and I tried to run off thinking no one understood me, but as a mother who's had to deal with her own troubled child, I so get it. He was probably trying to figure out what happened to his daughter and how he could get me back. When I finally did leave my house to join my boyfriend and "the Muslims," the one person's face I recall was my papa. My family at the time sat down for dinner like nothing was happening. I just remember seeing his face trying not to look me in the eye, acting like everything was good. I could tell that deep down, he was suffering. Since I stayed in touch with my mother, I used to see my father from time to time. When he purchased the new house, he took me to see it, and when they finally moved in, he tried to get me to come back home. At the time I eventually made it there, I was already pregnant, and my friend and a cult member was with me. I desperately wanted to come back home, but I was still deeply tied to "the Muslims," plus being knocked up, I knew it wouldn't be an option. I made up my mind to return home by the time I was five months pregnant, but the only thing that stood in my way was my father. Being 21 and pregnant was not part of his plan for me, so I knew he wouldn't welcome me with open arms. My mother, who was well aware of the situation, decided to tell papa the bad news. She later revealed to me that he told her I needed to get rid of the "wretched thing." She'd explain to him that I was too far along to terminate and that I wanted to come home. My mother always said she never forgot papa walking back and forth around the house, standing still and in shock. Since I grew frantic with wanting to go home, I called home crying frequently. The last time I called my mother to let me speak to papa, I blurted out. I was pregnant with tears running down my face. His powerful voice filled with emotion told me to come home. Once I got my father's approval to come home, I didn't even let two days pass, and I returned back to my family. When I finished globing my dinner down like a starved savage, my father spoke to me, trying to figure out how I got myself in this fucked situation. He kept telling me over and over that I lost so much time and that I should be finishing school instead of being in this unfortunate mess. Since I wasn't eating right, I must not have been showing cause he nearly jumped off the couch when I revealed how far along I was. In the next few months, we went through an array of emotions within our household. Happy and thankful that I returned, but disappointed, angry, and saddened that I returned in this state. To make matters worse, my papa was under the illusion that I was married. In his mind, there was no way that I could be so depraved and have a baby out of wedlock. When we talked further about my predicament, he said that he needed my marriage certificate so that he can have it annulled. Can you even picture the heart-wrenching anxiety I had to deal with having to tell my precious papa that I wasn't married? That I was the thing he wanted to avoid; pregnant, uneducated, and unwed. I honestly can't recall word for word what he said, but I do know he was furious about this catastrophe. At one point, I recall him telling me he felt like killing himself. Having this big, strong man that I always could count on no matter what tell me this and knowing that I was responsible for him feeling this way almost put me on the edge. I wanted to die myself rather than hurt him. Despite his revelation, he put his feelings aside to try and help me. Knowing my papa as I did, I now realize that was one of the hardest things he had to deal with. His only child in such a condition and him not revealing his true feelings to the full extent for my sake. It didn't take balls to do that, it took heart. When he came into my room with a gleam in his eye and a smile to get me so we could enjoy a nighttime snack together, the love he felt for me overshadowed his disappointment and was deeply felt when he danced with me and my big belly and especially when he found me crying, realizing I wasn't ready for my impending motherhood,. At eight and half months pregnant, he came home from work to find my face covered in tears as I revealed to him I now realized I fucked up my life. All he could do was agree, of course, but he took me out for a drive. We ended up going to a local Catholic church. By ending up there, he was trying to get me back to my old life.

When my labor pains started, he and my mother drove me to the hospital around midnight. Though I wasn't dilated and was told I could have my baby in another two days or two weeks, so I went through my labor pains by myself at home. When it got to the point that I couldn't take it anymore, I went into my parents' room, and my father instructed me on how to breathe. My mother revealed to me that he told her as he left for work that morning with tears in his eyes, saying, why did I have to get myself into this situation. He didn't like to see me suffer. Despite my doctor's prediction, I gave birth the next day. The first person I called and informed was my father. When my family came to visit me, my mother was over the moon with the baby, while my father stood reserved with his face in a somewhat scowl. The baby being here now would be the real hurdle. His expression softened as I revealed the baby's name, Georgia, after my grandmother and his mother. It was my way of saying thank you for everything he had done for us. When I finally went home, my father approached me, revealing everything he felt but kept bottled up. He also said how he had wished I had a boy because I would have to be extra careful dating/finding a suitable mate with a girl child. As we spoke, my mother joined the conversation while trying to dissuade the situation by commenting on how the baby looked like her namesake, which made him smile. Though he didn't hold Georgia, he didn't like holding newborns, he would come in and check on her when she cried and tried to comfort her. Thus, he began his attachment and affection for this little girl who he would come to view as his own. He even put her on his insurance in order for her to get the proper medical care. Due to this, I gave a speech at her baptism reception, where I singled out both my parents for all they did for me. In front of his friends and peers, I stated that he was the living definition of a good father, which left everyone in tears. After the festivities, I recall seeing him hold and kiss Georgia for the first time. As we adjusted to our new family life, there was some controversy. Hakeem, in his drug-induced haze, would call requesting to speak to my father. He claimed he wanted to marry me and would only accept my father's word on the matter. Papa answered the phone angrily, telling him never to call the house again. Undeterred, he persisted till he got the dial tone. When Hakeem was killed, papa was totally indifferent to the situation, which may seem cold, but for him, this young man was an intruder who disturbed his world by influencing me to leave my life and everything I knew to be nothing more than a baby momma.

One condition of my moving back was that I enroll back in college after my baby's birth and that I get a job. Since I wasted my time and his money when I last went to school, he told me I would finance my education this time around. He said since I was a single mother, I would apply for financial aid and school loans. In the fall of 1993, I had enrolled back in school but was still not fully prepared to apply myself to my studies. I was dealing with the death of my ex-boyfriend/child's father, balancing motherhood and having a life. Since papa wouldn't give me any money for myself (only for the baby), I got a part-time job at a retail bank nearby. Adding that to the equation, I didn't do very well in my first semester. I enrolled full time and ended up dropping a class and passing only two classes. When he saw my report card, he was beyond pissed. He told my mother that if I didn't get myself together, I wouldn't be able to continue living at home. I think at the time, it scared me, but not enough to fully straighten up. To be honest, I was more interested in getting laid than my education. Fortunately, I eventually started focusing on getting my brain right instead of my🐱 and got it together after two semesters.

Once I was focused on school, our relationship improved a hell of a whole lot. He would help me to continue to keep my academic stride by watching and playing with a then-toddler Georgia so that I could study. When I had to take French in order to fulfill a requirement, he helped me as well. Even though I spoke fluent French when I was younger, I lost it as I got older. To this day, I still get it jumbled with the creole. I had to write an assignment for class and couldn't write in French. He helped me to write the letter to T and assisted with the pronunciations. Either as he got older, he mellowed out, or the fact that I was actually taking an interest in my learning did it because he was no longer the big scary figure ready to go off on me for one little mistake. Once I started exclusively dating my future husband, I became even more serious about my studies and got my life in order. I recall one time while I was driving home, I started thinking about everything I went through with Hakeem, the religion, and what I put my parents through. I got home and found my papa sitting down in the kitchen. I went and sat on his knee and told him I promised to rectify everything, and I did. Shortly after, I got my associate's degree and moved to a four-year university. The one person who congratulated me was papa. He called me from work to let me know that he was proud of me. When things got serious with darling hubby, I started to let papa know about him. The first thing he asked about was his education. Haitians and education are like white rice and *sòs pwa*[27], they go together. To demonstrate how much he valued it when I was in the muck of my pregnancy situation, as he was yelling about Hakeem. He said that he would never accept him even if he graduated from Harvard University. When I told papa hubby wasn't college-educated but had a good job and supported me in acquiring mine, he didn't push against it. I guess he felt that I was happy, being treated right, focused on my education, and with a Haitian, it was all good. He eventually met him on Mother's Day 1996 when he came bearing roses for me, and my father nodded his approval. A year later, hubby and my family were all with me as I graduated with my bachelor's. My father embraced me with tears in his eyes. When we got home, he opened an old bottle of champagne that he had been saving for this occasion and took everyone out to dinner to celebrate. The next day the festivities continued with the party where I once again honored and thanked my parents in a speech for helping me reach this milestone in my life. The party really got going when I started the first dance with my favorite and best dance partner, my papa. I'll never forget the fact that his face was plastered with a permanent smile the whole evening. The celebrations continued five months later when I was engaged. When I called him at work to let him know, he said teasingly, "You gonna leave me?" I told him I would never leave him. By November, hubby and I married civilly and he moved into my family home. Papa fully welcomed him in. He used to call my father Doc and papa told him, "Do

---

[27]sòs pwa-bean sauce

not call me Doc, call me Pop." During his speech at our wedding reception, he addressed him as my son, and everyone applauded. When we took a father-daughter pic, I started tearing up. I cried out of happiness because at this moment, I knew we were both so happy and had come so far… To know that five years ago, I came back home in shame and disgrace. Now I was a college graduate, getting married, and celebrating with my family and friends I had once abandoned. It was a miracle. Thanks to a 12-week fetus known as Cassie, I couldn't fully enjoy my wedding. My father, however, enjoyed himself immensely. He was drunk with joy and alcohol. He danced all night long. At one point during our father-daughter dance, he asked me if I was happy with "my party." Just like he always did when I was little.

Six months later, we welcomed a new little life into our lives. Cassandra Marie's birth was the total opposite of Georgia's. Papa still adopted his policy of not holding newborns, but instead of a scowl, he had a smile. Not saying he loved Georgie any less, but the fact that Cassie was the product of marriage made it more of a reason to celebrate. We had offered him the role of godfather, but he declined, suggesting (well, more like insisting) his godson, whose father is my godfather and papa's best friend. He wanted to keep the tradition going. Dealing with the after-effects of childbirth, I had the baby blues. At one point, I was crying, and he asked my mother what was wrong. She told him and he came to talk to me. I told him that I wasn't sure how I would be able to take care of two children now. He answered the age-old Haitian saying, "*Manman deux petit kounye a mete fanm sou kò,*" meaning you're the mother of two, so now you just got to be a woman about it and deal with it.

Unfortunately, my baby blues added with lack of sleep brought out some bad and repressed memories that I had, particularly regarding my dentist. I mentioned before that my dentist was a very cruel man who physically abused me. Whenever I had any medical appointments, my father would take me since he was the only one at the time who could drive. It was just always him and I in all of my pediatrician appointments. We would take that long drive and then go to Arthur's

Treachers to get fish and chips as a treat. Regardless of whether I got vaccines, it ended up good. I thought the dentist's office would be no different. I went there for the first time at six years old. He seemed very nice, and he even let me choose which toothpaste flavor I wanted to use for my cleaning. I looked forward to the next visit, but it turns out that I had two cavities that had to be attended to. Despite him explaining that he would numb the area with a needle, I panicked when he approached me with it. I felt the sting of the needle, and I retaliated by screaming and pushing the lamp above me. The dentist didn't like it one bit and told my father to leave the room which he did. I still remember calling for him and telling him not to leave me, but he did. The dentist then said that he was gonna fix my cavity without the use of NOVOCAINE, so it would really hurt. I don't recall my reaction or even the pain. I just recall feeling abandoned and let down by my papa. Despite his sadistic tendency, I continued to be seen by this man throughout the duration of my childhood and adolescence. The one time he severely left his mark was when my mother took me, but I'll get into that when I discuss her.

Whenever I brought the situation up to friends, everyone would ask the same question which I asked myself. How come your father didn't protect you?? For years and even now, I've struggled with this, and the only excuse that is even tolerable is the African proverb of "It takes a village to raise a child." My parents believed that other people had the right to discipline me. In fact, most Haitians usually do. The only time my godfather spanked me was when I was around four or five in front of my father because I told him I would be a cigarette smoker when I grew up. Even darling hubby had said on several occasions when he was growing up that if his father's friends saw him outside misbehaving, they had the right to remove their belts and start hitting him. Papa emphatically agreed with this approach. But this dentist was obviously unhinged, and he ended up taking advantage of my father's demeanor to do his dirty work. I mean, how do you become so disturbed to the point of inflicting pain on a child due to a scream and hitting a lamp? My youngest once pushed her doctor. Hubby and I took her due to a sore throat. She must have been four or five years old at the time. When he examined her tonsils with the tongue dispenser, it went down far. Baby girl pushed him back with all fierceness, and do you know what his reaction was? He just laughed it off with hubby and said, "wow she's feisty." I felt that my father didn't want to be a troublemaker. He had that aristocratic French/Haitian manner that you didn't make trouble or waves, particularly when this was someone that was recommended to him via a friend. Also, he probably viewed the dentist as an associate and would never do anything to disrespect him, even if it included defending me. It's funny after he passed away, my mother and I were debating whether to pursue a lawsuit against his doctor. But my mother, quoting my father, said, "Doctors don't sue doctors."

Though moving in with my family was a good idea in the beginning, it was something I started to regret. As a nineteen-year-old college student living at home, my cousin Waldo once said, "Three adults can't live together." His words were nothing but the truth. Being a wife and mother, I was still treated as a daughter. So, I was reprimanded for whatever I did, even if it was something so slight. I came home from work once after getting my hair done. During dinner, my cousin noticed and complimented me. Papa had a kanpcion and started yelling at me in front of everyone, stating, why did I need to get my hair done? SMH. The persistent scolding wasn't the only thing, I had to deal with his anger regarding our living arrangement. Many thought that when we moved in, we used to provide my parents with some monetary compensation for the household. Well, we didn't provide a "gaddam" thing, and it was totally fucked up on both our parts. Papa refused to ask hubby for something that he felt should have naturally been done. But as time went by, he got older, he got tired, and he got frustrated at the insensitivity. He never took out his anger on hubby, so I was the scapegoat. At one point, he got so mad at me that he took an open bag of rice and poured it over my head. Though I remained calm, I was furious and later took out my anger on hubby. Speaking of which, whenever I fought with him (which was a lot), my father never got involved, but when things got out of hand, all he had to do was loudly call out my name in order to try and calm me down. It was around this time that I was truly fed up with my life and hubby, so I decided to return to school in order to provide myself and my girls the life we deserved. I also realized that if I was gonna salvage the relationship I had with my parents, I needed a place of my own. So, I worked towards fulfilling my dreams. Once I graduated, I was determined to turn my life around. Unfortunately, I got a rude awakening from life when everything I set out to do crumbled. It was during this time that I was let go from a second job. I didn't mention this before out of embarrassment, but right after I was unceremoniously removed from my temp job, I got another job at an insurance company as an HR administrator, but I let the anxiety of the job and being unable to find employment get to me to a point that I was fired. When I told my father about it, he almost passed out. It was at this point he saw that education in America was not valued as before.

Things went from bad to worse when hubby lost his job as well. We became completely dependent on my father who was dealing with his own issues with work. By this time, papa had reduced his work from three jobs to two. But eventually, it went down to one and then none. See, papa was one of those old-fashioned men who believed in working harder, not smarter theory. He also believed that his hard work would reward him so that he and my mother would be taken care of in their old age. However, he too was in for a rude awakening. He believed so deeply in the work system that would provide for him in exchange for his time and dedication that he was shocked when one job he devoted 19 years let him go in order to avoid providing him with his pension. As far as the other two jobs are concerned, I don't know the full story, but I do know that a man who spent his whole life working his ass off for his family and his/their future ended up being kicked to the curb and sorely discouraged. It was during this time that I now realized my papa was depressed. Resigned, he started playing solitaire on our home computer on a day-to-day basis. By this time, the mortgage payments had ballooned from $3000 to $6000, and some change. My parents did some kind of financing that didn't work in their favor. But with finances being at an all-time low, they were having trouble making payments. At one point, papa filed bankruptcy. My mother turned to my father, asking what they were supposed to do. Papa replied, *"Sa ou foute vle m 'fè,"* meaning what the hell do you want me to do. I so get it now. I don't and can't begrudge him. He worked long and hard all his life, played by the rules, doing right by his family and to have it all blown up in his face; it was so heartbreaking, especially when I started working at my bullshit collector job, and he would ask me for $20 bucks. I got so mad. But my reason for my anger had nothing to do with being selfish and wanting to keep my money to myself. Absolutely not. This man did right by me as a child and took care of me and my oldest daughter. At the time, he made sure my children and I were fed and sheltered; how could I not want to give back? I was upset that he was reduced to having to ask me for money. Despite this, we both shared the dream that we would get out of this mess. He was there for me when I lost my shit[28] in front of everyone about my situation and ended up crying hysterically. He calmly sat down next to me and talked about how our lives would be if we had the good fortune of a financial windfall. He was also there for me when my shitty booty job offered me a promotion by telling me with a smile 'go get your job'. He also fully supported me when I decided to separate from my hubby.

It was Mother's Day 2007, and I was very upset about my situation. Papa took us all out for brunch and saw how sad I was. He told me how much he loved me and said, "There isn't a father in the world that loves his child as much as he loves me." My poor papa had a lot to deal with during the last two years of his life. I think that contributed to his death as well. This was around the time my daughter was acting up. My father, GOD bless him, tried to intervene by disciplining her, but nothing helped. At one point, I had my daughter "arrested" and put in a psych ward for the weekend. Papa and my mother tagged along with me to the hospital that whole weekend. When she left for school in West Virginia, she was on the outs with my father. On my last Father's Day with him, I took him to church and brunch at the Cheesecake Factory, just the both of us. When we returned home, Georgia called to wish him a Happy Father's Day and he was so very happy. He truly looked forward to

---

[28] lost my shit-broke down

going to visit her at the school, but unfortunately, he never got a chance to. During this time, his health started failing. My father always had high blood pressure from the time I was a little girl. At one point, he was hospitalized for what was my seventh birthday. Again, as I mentioned my birthday, he didn't skip a beat by making sure I had my party at school instead since they couldn't at home. He was on medication from that time on. When he was dealing with my pregnancy and Hakeem, my mother always said it was by the grace of GOD he didn't develop a stroke. Due to the high blood pressure, his kidneys started to fail, and he had started doing dialysis home treatments. Also in 2007, he had his prostate removed due to cancer. In the summer of 2008, he started experiencing excruciating back pains that immobilized him. We had to contact darling hubby on two occasions to come home to help him off the floor. One time it happened that I came home to find him in his bathroom trying to pull himself up. He looked at me with all sadness saying, *"Mwen pa ka pran li anko,"* meaning he couldn't take it anymore. It truly broke my heart. After he passed on, I even shared this scenario with Georgie who was moved to heart-wrenching tears.

The weekend before papa was unknowingly hospitalized, he sat in his chair in the family room. I remember I had fallen asleep on the couch and woke up, later, to find him staring at me. The staring was unnerving at the time, but I think he knew his time was limited, and he was trying to hold on to my image. July 22nd, he was sitting at the kitchen counter again staring at me, but this time he took my hand stating, *"Eske ou konnen jan mwen renmen ou?"* Meaning "Do you know how much I love you?" I don't remember what my response was, but I didn't take it seriously. That early morning, the whole household awoke to hear my mother screaming, *"Francois mouri.... Leve, leve!!!"* Francois is dying .... wake up, wake up. Hubby went running to the room first, and I stood outside the door with my aunt, my father's younger sister. I'm sorry, but I can't tolerate illness in any way, shape, or form. Even if it's a loved one. That's why I never considered being a nurse, but if I had, it would be just for the money which means I would be a fucked-up nurse. Getting back to that early morning, I do recall looking in and seeing hubby calling out "Pop, Pop" removing the wires from the dialysis machine, and my mother trying to get a dazed and confused-looking papa to focus on her. When we got to a local hospital, we found out that he had a blood clot in his brain that ruptured, causing a seizure. He needed to be operated on immediately. Since they were not equipped, we ended up having to go to Long Island Jewish hospital. All of papa's close doctor friends came immediately and rallied by our side. My mother ended up staying the night while he was in surgery, and it looked like it was a success. When I saw and spoke to him for the last time, I told him how much I loved him, and he replied with some difficulty that he loved me too. Thinking everything was good, I returned to work. Then later, I got the call from my aunt that my mother called from the hospital saying that my father suffered a stroke. Immediately after they removed the tube from his throat, they fed him some soup which caused him to choke, then vomit and led to said stroke. Things became worse when at one point during the night, it didn't look like he was gonna make it. That whole time I tried to keep strong for my mother's sake and even my own but seeing a team of doctors and nurses working on your father who even though you knew was fading, but thinking he had a fighting chance really affected me to the point that I started shaking uncontrollably. Though he lived through the night, he slipped into a coma. From that moment on, I lived at the hospital, taking a leave of absence from work. I was such a permanent fixture there that a nurse, who wasn't even dealing with my father's case, saw me crying about the situation. I was just all-out exhausted physically and mentally. She brought me hospital footies, though I didn't catch her name, but the gesture really meant something to me. At one point, I got tired of sleeping in the waiting room. I went and slept in my car in the parking lot which a lot of people warned me not to continue doing. Despite the prognosis, my papa's good friend, Dr. Verdier, and I refused to accept the inevitable. He even came by to test his reflexes. Due to papa's reactions, we saw and had hope that he would make it. My father awoke from his coma, but we were told he would never be the same. He was then moved from ICU to the Palliative Care Unit.

The day we were told papa was dying, the one thing that stuck out in my mind was that I didn't have any underwear. Thinking I would find some low-key store in the area, little did I know I would drive over to the next town's Macy's to purchase black silk panties. It's almost like foreshadowing the death and mourning that would come. Once I got my underwear, my mother and hubby came specifically to meet with the doctors who told us that his organs were failing and there was nothing else that could be done. I recall the medical social worker came and sat with me due to my stoic reaction. I started going off about how fucking unfair life was, running down the list of bad in my life, and now my father was dying. My mother was inconsolable at this point, and as we entered his room, he just stared straight ahead. I shared this with someone who said my father was looking at the journey he had ahead of him. I continued staying with my father, this time in his room. They had a couch-like bed where I slept during the night to be awakened to the many nurses who had to bathe/change him. At one point, he saw me and looked at me like a baby giving me a smile. Even the nurses commented on how he recognized me. Living at the hospital took its toll on me. It got to a point that on August 24th, I could no longer take sleeping on that ward of death with its sickeningly nauseous sweet smell. I spoke with the doctor that night who told me my papa would be alright, and I went to sleep nearby at my mother-in-law's place. When I got to her house, I passed out so hard that I didn't hear my cell phone ring. My mother-in-law who was up and getting ready to leave for work, had to tell me my phone rang. When I called back the number, it was the hospital telling me my father had just died. For almost a month, I stayed with papa day and night; the one time I wasn't there , that was when he chose to pass. Whenever I tell anyone this, everyone says he loved me more than anything because he didn't want me to see him go. A friend of my mother's even predicted that saying 'papa saw me sitting there watching him stating he would wait for the one moment when I wasn't there, and that would be when he would go'.

Planning my father's funeral was a real eye-opener. Going down the stairs in the funeral home basement with my mother and picking out caskets was surreal. It's like the person is still with you till you realize they must be buried. Since my mother and father's money was involved, the funeral was done in style. Again, I mention I have no brothers or sisters, so I organized the whole shebang. I arranged the limousine seating, made sure the funeral programs were printed with directions, put together the pallbearers, and chose the music for the wake which included Luther Vandross *"Dance with My Father."* The one area my mother put her foot down was for the wake; she refused to have it done on separate days the way it was usually done. She didn't want to prolong the grief process any further. She wanted everything that same day done and over. My first reaction upon seeing him was that he didn't look like himself. Something was definitely off, and I realized they tucked in his lower lip. In my previous chapter, I mentioned my underbite, but I failed to mention that I got it from my papa who got it from his father. My mother used to say, *"Mzemai bouch Mte. Thebaud gate figi pitit mwen.* Meaning my grandfather's jaw ruined her child's face. After viewing him, I made my hubby promise to make sure that they didn't botch my mouth up when my time comes. Seeing papa in the coffin was already distressing, but what really made me cry out loud was when his older brother saw him. I'm very sentimental, so I envisioned my father's birth and his brother probably being told by his parents, you have to watch over your baby brother, and now his younger brother was gone before him. My crying continued when members of his medical school stood by the coffin and announced that they were the graduating class of 1965, sending home one of their own. One man you could clearly see was visibly ill, walking with a cane and drooling, but he stood up there, resilient and all. During the burial at the cemetery, all his friends and colleagues went into an uproar when they sealed the tomb due to the fact that it plainly said his name without the title 'doctor' in front. In the back of my mind, I thought that where he is now doesn't matter what he was, but as I got back to my reality there, I promised to make sure to add that acronym.

After the dead have been blessed and buried, so begins the hard part of trying to live a normal life. How does one go back to normal when the past two months you've lived your life with the hope that you would be wheeling your father out of the hospital in a wheelchair instead of the funeral that took place? I imagined his head bandaged up like a swami, wearing his gray bomber jacket hubby got him and his large white reebok sneakers. But you just go on, especially since I had my mother to look after now.

The fall of 2008 brought about the presidential election which my papa was so proud of Barack winning the democratic nomination. At the time, I, unfortunately, cast a shadow of doubt for him when I mentioned that I didn't think that a black man would ever be elected as president. I was going through my own fucked up issues in life, causing my negative feelings to spill over into everything. When the election day came, I couldn't pass up the moment and not share it with my father, so I made sure to take out his picture when I cast my vote for Obama. Due to this, a part of me always wanted to meet former President Obama for my father's sake. With Obama winning and serving two terms, you would have thought that I expressed my desire to meet him sooner than later, but I did eventually send the following letter below:

Dear Mr. President,

I hope this letter finds you and your beautiful family well. Allow me to introduce myself. My name is Sybil Thebaud-Brierre, I am a 45-year-old African-American female, and I am requesting a meeting in person with you and your lovely wife on behalf of my beloved father and myself. All daddy's girls think that their fathers are great, and I can honestly say mine was. My father was a physician who came from Haiti to make a better life for himself and his family in America. Growing up as a child of Caribbean parents, education was severely stressed. My father made sure I received a good education by enrolling me in Catholic school from the time I was in first grade. Papa loved learning and was very intelligent. My mother used to say that you could tell my father was intelligent because of his large ears which incidentally were similar to yours. I remember one time finding a book among one of his belongings about how to speak and write Latin and sharing it with a friend of mine who said my father was a "learned man." When I graduated from high school, I recall my principal asked my father if he was proud. My father said yes, but this was just the beginning. Unfortunately, I didn't take the straight and narrow path to college. I wandered off from my home, family, and friends with a less than desirable boyfriend and found myself unwed and pregnant. Despite my inappropriate predicament, my parents welcomed me with open arms. One of my conditions upon my return was that I go back to school. After the birth of my daughter, I enrolled at the State University of New York at Farmingdale. During that time, my parents helped to raise my daughter so I could focus on school full time. There were times my father, after a full day of work, would help watch my daughter so I could study/write papers for school. After getting off to a rocky start, I got my Associate degree in Liberal Arts and transferred to the State University of Stony Brook, where I graduated a year in advance in 1997 with a Bachelor's Degree in Psychology and a minor in Africana Studies. I eventually married and had another child returning to Stony Brook in 2002. I got my Masters of Professional Studies in Human Resource Management in 2003, graduating with a 3.7 GPA. My father cried tears of joy that his little girl not only triumphed from her circumstance, but she excelled. Alas, my education did not help me find suitable and long-lasting employment; in fact, there was a time when I was unemployed for over a year. When I did find employment, I was gravely underemployed. It was during that terrible time I found myself working as a bill collector for an oil company. I was depressed and angry at the world regarding my circumstances. In June 2008, right after you won the Democratic Nomination, my father came up to me saying what an accomplishment it was. He was so proud you would have thought it was his own son. I remember shooting down his pride with my pessimistic, defeatist attitude by posing the rhetorical question, 'did he think America was going to elect a black man as president?' Regrettably, my father never got a chance to see your victory. My father passed away in August 2008. Which is why I am writing this letter now. I know it's the 11th hour with your administration ending soon, but I would like to meet you in person for my father's sake and mine. For me, meeting you, the first African

*American male President of the United States of America, would mean
I made amends to my father, myself, and you.*

Most Respectfully

But alas, I got one of those lovely little thank you cards from the White House, meaning it was just put to the side.

It's been almost 10 years now, and not a day goes by that I don't think of my papa. He was my biggest champion when I went to Las Vegas on my first girl's trip. Hubby went on two guy's trips at one point. One of the trips was to Vegas under the guise that "we" would be moving there, and he was checking it out. What was supposed to be a weekend trip ended up being a two-week outing. My father was like; he's gone on vacation without you, why shouldn't you? He was my comforter as I cried when I experienced my first real bout with racism as the guest at a lily-white sweet sixteen. The birthday girl had a Black boyfriend, and they shared a special dance. During her dance, a "friend" at the time made some disturbing comments forgetting that I was at the table. She did eventually realize I was there, and as she gave a half-hearted apology, I jumped in without skipping a beat, trying to act as if nothing happened. In fact, I added insult to injury by agreeing with her and adding my own two cents into making a joke that brought down my race. To this day, I hate myself for that. Any who, trying to laugh it off, I could not hide the hurt and shame I felt especially when I shared it with pops. He wiped my tears and hugged me. He was my unusual supporter when I had my first real panic attack as I took my SAT and called him crying because I couldn't complete the test. Instead of the usual yelling when it came to education and learning, I got a calm, soothing voice telling me don't worry; everything would be okay. Again, he surprised me as I got older by comforting me with my pigeon phobia. When I was younger, it was a source of embarrassment and anger for him. I ruined many outings due to this. But one time, as we went to the market, there was a large pigeon perched on the sign. I got a little anxious and he kindly told me to hold on to him and not pay attention to it. He was my initiator and to this day, responsible for my love of the *Star Wars*

Franchise. From 1977 to 1985, we went just us two, and now as I watch the new movies, I think of him fondly... He was my enabler when it came to food and the reason why I am a foodie. Any time we went out and were on our way home, I would whine till I got my way which involved stopping at Carvel or Dunkin Donuts. To celebrate getting our first VCR and recording *Star Wars,* he brought me 20 White Castles, 10 with cheese, and 10 without. Hubby always teases me about being a "fat kid" at heart cause Lord knows I love to eat, and papa contributed to my slight obsession with food. Whether it was Pizza Hut, Burger King, Mickey D's, and Haitian take out he would get it for me. The only time he stopped "feeding" me was after Georgia was born. I was 30 lbs. overweight and just started dieting. That Valentine's Day, instead of the usual box of chocolates, he gave me a card-shaped in the form of a chocolate bon bon to encourage me to continue with my battle of the bulge.

He was and still is my protector since he has visited me once or twice via my dreams; telling me he loves me and will always be with me; also, warning me as well about my drinking. I never was a big drinker till I went to Jamaica and stayed at an all-inclusive resort with hubby, courtesy of my father, of course. Liquor was served from 10 am till whenever. Well, I had a drink here and there. It really became more consistent, especially after I lost both parents. So, he showed up in my dream, shaking his finger at me saying, *"Ou bwè twop."*

The one place I never thought I would see my papa again is in my grandson. The first male in our family resembles my father. From the first time I saw him at three months old, I told my daughter he looked like papa. Now that he has teeth, he has the "Thebaud Trademark" of a slight underbite. But regardless of his teeth, everyone from my pharmacist to family members has said that they see the similarities in his facial structure

Having him in my life and seeing my father's face is an additional blessing. Reminding me that life indeed does go on.

MANMAN

"Don't go crying to your mama"

"Cause you're on your own in the real world"

Paramore *"Ain't it Fun"*

Someone once told me after my father passed away that the pain that I felt was strong, but it would not be as strongly felt as when my mother would pass. Thinking that I would have some time with her and wouldn't be experiencing it for quite a while, I tried not to focus on it. But thinking back to when my cousin lost her mother to cancer, and I was discussing it with my parents. I said losing your mother at nineteen must be very hard. My father, whose mother was dead for some ten years, replied, "losing your mother at any age is hard."

Anne Marie Jacqueline Desroches, going only by Jacqueline, was born April 19, 1941, in Cap-Haitien, Haiti, the third and last daughter of my grandmother. My grandparents were married, but my grandfather had done something that warranted him leaving the country for his safety, so my grandmother raised her three daughters with her spinster sisters and her mother. I've mentioned color/hair complex, and I have to say that my mother was an expert on that matter. She was heavily influenced by her surroundings, particularly my great grandmother. She was Dominican born with light skin, pointy European nose, green eyes, and long straight black hair. She hated my grandmother's choice for a husband because he was Black. The fact that he had to leave my grandmother didn't make it any better. My great grandmother didn't like my mother or her older sister, Jeannie because they looked more like my grandfather and had kinky hair. She tended to favor the older sister Rose because she had "good long hair." My mother would say that she and Jeannie would stare out the window as their grandmother dressed up Rose and took her to church because she was considered the beauty. SMH. Thus, therefore my mother came to love long hair. She always made a big deal out of mine and my younger daughter's hair. She said that the reason I had come out with such pretty hair was because of the mixture of DNA from her grandmother and my father who had "good hair." To point out how much my mother loved good hair, I recall one time when my parents were debating where to go on vacation and my father mentioned Africa. My mother was adamant that she would never want to visit it saying, *"sa Africa fè pou m'wen eksepte ban mwen tèt grenn,"* meaning what has Africa done for me except giving me this nappy ass hair. SMH. Even though she had kinky herself she hated her hair. If someone had very nappy hair my mother would say *"ti tèt li grennnnn grennnn,"* she'd drag it out to emphasize how nappy the person's hair was. Ta, as my kids would call her and I eventually followed, was a real connoisseur of color and could categorize every type of black person. A light skin girl with nappy hair or little to no hair is *"vye grimèl."* A light skin girl with long hair is a *"grimèl deluxe."* A dark skin girl with good hair and good features, she would say was a *"marabou."* She even applied her ideology of color to my children stating that if Georgia was in Haiti, they would address her in creole because she had very nappy hair. As opposed to Cassandra who at the time was light skin and had long hair, would be addressed in French. She was also dead set on what she considered a mulatto, particularly in Haiti. She said that the Haitian mulatto and mulatress were up to par compared to the American ones. One time we were watching a reality TV show, a girl came on and I told her that it was a mulatress. She said with vexation, "That's a mulatress??!!" No way, the ones in Haiti can pass for Italian or Spanish, they don't even look like they are Black when you see them.

Ta met my father working as a secretary for the Haitian government. My father came in to get something typed and begged my mother to do it for him. She said that when she saw how big and tall, he was, she told her best friend at the time that he looked like he was married but thank goodness he wasn't. My mother said on their first date that he tried to put his hand on her thigh, and she pushed it away. This is how my mother would say, 'Papa knew she was wife material because she didn't give it up right away'. They continued to date for some time before they got married in 1968, on her birthday. She said my father would say that his birthday gift to her was himself through marriage. They spent their honeymoon at my aunt's house with my then four-year-old cousin sleeping in the middle between them. Within the following months, they made their move to the United States. My mother always said that she valued my father for getting all her paperwork in order and bringing her to America with him. While here, she worked full time until she became pregnant. Getting pregnant wasn't easy for her. When they first married, they took precautions because he said he didn't want any children any time soon. However, at the boarding house where they resided, my father loved playing with my older cousin who was a baby at the time. Many of her friends would tell her that regardless of what he says, his actions speak louder. They advised her to hurry up and get on the baby-making train. So, my mother stopped taking her pills but still found out that she wasn't pregnant. So, she went to an OB-Gyn who did some testing on her fallopian tube using gas to see if they were blocked. This ended up unblocking them. Whenever we got into our arguments, she would always bring this up as a way of trying to make me feel guilty. Saying how much she suffered from that test in order to have me. She also used to say that the reason she had so much digestive gas was because of this. SMH. My mother also did a special novena to get pregnant by going to a particular St. Anthony's Church in Manhattan for several days. By November 1970, my mother became pregnant. Ta said that there were two things she craved constantly while pregnant with me: White Castle burgers and Carvel ice cream. One time my father forgot to bring them for her, and she cried like a baby. That definitely explains my love of Carvel and hamburgers being my favorite American food.

My mother said that she adored and loved taking care of me as a baby. It was something that I think was innate in her because I eventually saw this with both my children. She loved dressing me up and putting little ribbons in my hair. She said that my hair was so "*swah*"[29] that she was

---

[29]swah- Haitian Creole for soft, silky hair

able to put Shirley Temple curls naturally. At one point, she took me to the pediatrician, and he told her, "Mrs. Thebaud stop pressing the baby's hair." She let him know with indignation that she never did that, and my hair was naturally like that. Again, Ta and the hair.

Growing up Ta was a fulltime housewife and mother. She was devoted to my father and me. I know my mother did want to have more children, but as soon as I was born my father gave her birth control pills telling her he didn't want her to have a gaggle of kids like her sister Jeannie who had six. My parents did attempt to try and have another baby at one point and my mother was pregnant, but unfortunately, she lost the baby at 12weeks. Coming back from the supermarket at the insistence of my father, she lifted a heavy bag of rice and started bleeding right away. My mother said that papa was one of those males who hated to see females use pregnancy as an excuse or illness. After the miscarriage, they never attempted to have any more children. She soon saw that I was a handful.

Ta not only spoiled me, but she was very overprotective of me as well. She used to say *"yon sel grennje mwen gen,"* meaning she only had one eye and she had to look out for it. She made sure that she was always with me. In fact, when I first started school and had to take the school bus home, I cried and cried feeling lost without her. Another area that affected me was language. When I first went to school everyone was speaking English and I didn't understand. My mother didn't speak English very well, so since I was with her daily, we communicated in French and creole. The nursery school I attended suggested to my father that I watch TV to learn how to speak English. That suggestion soon became my downfall when it came to school. I loved to watch TV more than anything. So, instead of doing homework or studying, I'd be in front of the television set. Which brings me to education, just like papa, Ta was disappointed with me when it came to my grades. She would always compare me to others regarding my studies, and the way I applied myself. One time, a second-grade schoolmate Martine Jean came home with me when I was in first grade. When I got home the first thing I did was go straight to the kitchen, eat, and watch TV. Well,

Martine Jean did her homework first and it was only after she had completed all her work that she sat to eat and watch TV. After Martine left, Ta said over and over, "Why can't you be like her?" Focusing on my studies first. I provided the answer that most self-help gurus and probably GOD HIMSELF would agree and want; 'That I am who I am, and Martine Jean is who she is. The answer that no Haitian parent wants to hear. From then on until I was 38 years, my mother always reminded me of this scenario implying that I was wrong being myself. One thing I must mention about ole school Haitian parents is that individualism is not encouraged. They want you to be like everyone else and follow the "right" crowd.

I, like most creative kids, was horrible at math. Most of my grades in math were failing and beyond. If I got a 75 or 80, I thought I did well, but not my parents. Well, one time I got a hundred plus on my test, my math teacher was pulling out bonus points from his ass. Well, my best friend Monique got five points higher than me. I was so happy that I shared my joy with my mother as I showed her my exam and told her Monique's grade as well. Instead of praising my efforts and encouraging me for the future, do you know she was pissed at me for letting Monique beat me? At the time it was no secret. Monique wasn't the sharpest tool in the bunch, so Ta was severely disappointed that I let her get over on me.

My mother was very indulgent and tolerant when it came to me. I'm gonna admit something I've never admitted out loud before, I slept in my parents' room till I was around 17 years old. Now, let me clarify before people's minds start wandering about the sleeping arrangements. From the time I was a little girl till maybe 10 /11, I slept in the same bed with my parents. By the time I was 12, I slept on a pull-out mattress in front of the bed until I started driving. It was only when I got older and was married did, I realize what a cockblocker[30] I was. I even apologized to my mother for that when I had to deal with my younger daughter trying to sleep with hubby and me. But like most daughters, I did enjoy

---

[30] cock blocker-preventing sex from happening

sleeping with my mother just when it was both of us. Especially when papa worked late or didn't come home at all. Those days would be Wednesdays, Fridays, and Saturdays. As I got older, we had a bed with a trundle in my father's study that was used when I had sleepovers. Sometimes my mother and I would sleep there and make it like a sleepover. Ta was so gullible and easy to trick at times. One time as she got ready to sleep in the office with me, I took two pillows and one of her hairpieces so she would think I was already in bed. Once she came into the room, she locked the door. While I was outside of the room, I heard her talking to "me" as she got in the bed. Trying to stifle my laughter I knocked on the door real loud. I heard her talk to "me" in panic, then I knocked again, and she replied *"Ki moun Ki la*?!!! Who's there? I knocked again and she yelled *"Ki moun Ki foute la?*!!!!"Who the fuck is there?!! I burst out laughing hysterically. Even as I write this, I am collapsing in giggles. Whenever I repeated the story to my cousin, he would ask her how she thinks that the robber would understand creole☺. Another thing I enjoyed on those three nights pops wasn't there was the nighttime soap operas Ta and I watched together. First came *Dallas* on Friday nights, then came *Dynasty* on Wednesday, and eventually *Falcon Crest* on Friday as well. I still remember the phenomenon of "Who Shot JR." Even though I now realize I was way too young for that type of programming at the time, I enjoyed those moments with my mother. Especially watching *Dynasty,* our love of all things glamorous and luxurious really came into play. We would watch just to see what the characters would be wearing. At one point, my mother had a dress designed and made simply because she saw it on Diahann Carroll's character of Dominique Deveraux. My mother was a true diva in every sense of the word.

When I started going to my new high school in Syosset, I let my mother know that some kids came to school in a limousine because their town didn't provide a school bus. So, when we went to the Mother-Daughter fashion show my mother decided she would rent a limo for the occasion. She said we had to show the *"blans"* these uppity whites; they weren't the only ones who had it like that. In fact, most times, she would rent a town car with a driver to pick me up if I had to stay after. My mother didn't learn to drive until I was around 13 or 14. When she did drive, she did it as rarely as possible so long as it wasn't too far. She was a very Nervous Nelly when it came to driving. When I was applying to high schools I naturally applied to my sister school, Sacred Heart Academy which was right around the corner from my elementary school, meaning that if I had to stay after, it would be no problem for my mother to pick me up. She could take the taxi, bus, or just drive. Well, when I didn't get in, naturally, due to my grades, not only was Ta upset, but she was also mad because she knew the hurdle and burden would be on her to pick me up if I had to stay after. So, when that happened, she always repeated over and over that my dumbass put her in this terrible position. One thing my mother did was never bite her tongue when it came to me.

In fact, she was very honest, especially when it came to my looks. She always told me that I wasn't the beauty of the family on my father's side. That title went to my older cousin who came out with her father's dark complexion and my aunt's classic features. Ta always used to say that when I was sixteen, she would get my nose fixed. From the time I was little till I was an adult; she always pinched my nose to try and make it straighter. She hated that I had a large flat Negroid nose. She wanted me to have a straight European nose. My father had an aunt who was an old maid, whom everyone used to say I looked like. My mother refused to acknowledge that because his aunt had the wide set nose she so despised. Even by herself, she would try to correct her nose by wearing her glasses on the tip to try and lift the shape of it. When I hit sixteen, I flat out refused to get rhinoplasty. Since I didn't get my nose done, my mother would always tell me that I needed to keep my hair long. Not only was it a plus as a black girl, but it helped to diminish the look of my nose. When I got the "haircut from hell" and I had my senior pictures taken, my mother said how ugly I looked in the pics. She complained so much about them that I ultimately had them redone.

When it came to dating, Ta tried to be as open-minded as possible, but was extremely challenged when it came to the guys I "dated." The first guy that came to the house was Steve. I mentioned before that he was my first kiss, and it took place in my living room with my mother not far away sitting in the kitchen nearby. Once Steve came over unexpectedly with his friend, Damian, she put her foot down, refusing to let me go with them when they suggested going to Mickey Ds. She said that if I even attempted to leave, she would call my father right then and there. She covered up for me regarding certain things with pops, but if I push things too far, she knew to play the "papa" card which would stop me from doing anything extreme or foolish. Now that I look back at that, I realize it was a smart move because she knew those guys had dishonorable intentions and were probably gonna run a train on me. As I mention, sex, she was very open to me about the subject. She didn't hide anything, but she did warn me that once you start, you can't stop. So, of course, she encouraged me to remain a virgin till I got married like "she did." Years later, she eventually revealed to me that they didn't wait till they were married, but she waited till they were engaged. While the rest of the house slept, she and papa did the do on the family sofa. I tried to keep my virginity, but once I had my first serious relationship, things changed. Once I told her I wanted to lose my virginity, she tried to discourage me. I remember at one point, a girlfriend of mine was trying to tell me not to do it in front of her, and she kept telling me to listen to her, but I refused. Exasperatedly, my mother gave me the money to go to Family Planning to make sure I took every precaution to avoid having a baby.

Since I was seeing Hakeem for almost a year, I thought the time came for my mother to meet him. That would be an experience I'd never forget. Like I explained before, Hakeem wasn't ugly, but he wasn't what ole school Haitians like my mother would deem an acceptable boyfriend. He met my mother wearing baggy jeans, an oversized shirt, his trademark hair in braids sticking straight up, and a nose ring. He was holding a brown paper bag with a drink inside. My mother later told me he looked like the "vagabonds[31]" she used to see at the bus terminal. Ta totally felt I could do so much better than Hakeem, and she never let me

---

[31]vagabond- a bum; degenerate

forget it. But since she saw he was a permanent fixture in my life, she tolerated him. She even would provide him with a hot and healthy meal. That's one thing my mother would never deny someone, a meal; whether she liked them or not, she always fed someone. Plus, she preferred that I was home with Hakeem instead of somewhere in the car. Unfortunately, worrying about where I would be became replaced by worrying about who I was when I transformed from a happy go lucky girl to the subservient wanna be "Islamic" wifey. No longer attending school, I was focused on breeding and distancing myself from my life. Ta tried to talk to me to see if she could get through to me, but I was too far gone to even listen. Once the time came for me to leave the house defeated but not down, she gave up the struggle and let me go on with the life I had chosen for myself. I continued to call her and made arrangements to see her as often as possible. During those visits, she would always provide me with money whether I needed it or not, and believe me, I did need it. As soon as I got pregnant, I shared what I thought was good news with her. She insisted that I get married immediately to avoid the shame of having a child out of wedlock. One time while my parents were in the process of moving, I went over to see my mother with Hakeem. She met us on the block in the car and went into a tirade telling him he had to marry me. He replied in a typical hood fashion that he didn't have to do anything. As I sat next to him smiling, my mother immediately left the car and ran home in tears. She would always repeat this situation to emphasize how hurt she was that I was this foolish young girl letting this guy "disrespect" me and thereby her.

Once I started getting frustrated with my situation, I called Ta daily to try and help me get out of it. Since she took into consideration that papa might not let me come back, she was prepared to make arrangements outside of the home in order to have somewhere safe for the baby and I. Fortunately, I was allowed back and the first thing my mother did was feed me a great big meal; something I hadn't enjoyed in quite a while. The following days she would take me clothes shopping for some much-needed maternity wear. My then dumbass, thinking everything was good, would try and talk as though nothing had really changed. I even tried sharing my baby's sono pics with her and pops at one point. She had to take me aside and reminded me that though I was back home, it wasn't exactly a happy occasion. I realized the scope of my actions when one night she angrily and tearfully shared how hurt she was that I forgot her birthday during my time away.

Every day I spent back home, I shared with her the details of my former fucked up life. I told her about how they beat up a friend and "cult member" because he was disrespectful to his mate; I told her about the ways of the "Lamb" and how I was ostracized because of my lack of cleaning skills. That last one eventually bit me in the ass because as a "Messy Marva," whenever I didn't clean up, she would constantly throw this in my face. That even the "community" couldn't tolerate me because I was such a slob. When we discussed Hakeem, I told her little by little what he had said/done to me. She wasn't upset, neither did she yell. One time, she got really upset when I told her he pulled my hair during an argument. She replied without missing a beat, "*Eske w se youn nan ki fè tèt li gran,*" translation was I responsible for the fact that he had nappy hair? But ,actually meaning his nappy-headed self had a lot of nerve attacking me. Talking about my relationship with her made me conclude that it wasn't good. She didn't outrightly tell me that but helped me to see for myself what the truth was. Due to this, we bonded again, especially as we shopped for the baby items. I truly cherish those moments we spent before the baby was born. We would spend our days shopping and going out to eat. After one of our excursions, we sat down to lunch, and the waiter asked me to repeat myself. Out of slight embarrassment and intimidation, I covered my mouth with my hand and started to repeat myself. My mother set me straight right then and there. She told me never to speak to anyone like that. Always have confidence!

When my baby was about to be born, it was my mother who trekked three times back and forth to the Dr's office/hospital; she held me as the contractions became too intense, and my mother who was with me as I gave birth to my little girl. She was one of the first people to hold her, and like any good mother, she was simply enamored. Despite the circumstances, she was a very proud grandmamma. The times she mentioned the baby's origin was when Hakeem came over. Although papa forbade me from having contact with him, Ta continued to allow it for my sake. When he first visited, she could not pass up the opportunity to remind him that the baby was illegitimate. She said, "You see your bastard!" He argued that she wasn't a bastard because he acknowledged her, but my mother was insistent about that because we were not married; the baby was a bastard. Even with me, my mother would share that Georgie's illegitimate origin was a very sore spot that deeply disturbed her. Ole school Haitians are very much into family history and family origin, so the fact that I broke the tradition and had a child out of wedlock was so not good. My mother explained to me that that's why my Aunt Marte treated me with such disdain because I brought upon this shame on the family.

Regardless of the situation, my mother was the best caretaker that Georgie and eventually Cassie would have. With her, I always knew my babies were safe. Georgie became a permanent fixture with my mother. Wherever my mother went, Georgie was always with her. Ta made it very clear that she would watch the baby for me as I got myself back together by going to school full time. She emphasized that since this fiasco, I had no other choice but to go up. She was always telling me that even though I made a mistake, my life wasn't over. I could still change my life for the better. Ta used to always say as long as there is life, there is hope; the only time one truly loses hope is when "*yo mete sa tag sou gwo zòtèy ou*" meaning you are lying in the morgue with that tag wrapped around your big toe.

When Hakeem was killed, my mother mourned him along with me. She went to the wake on my behalf and the funeral with me. Some people, actually his brother's first baby momma, was surprised that she was affected that way. Going so far as to say she thought my mother would be happy that he was dead. Ta never was someone who wanted to see anyone in a bad situation. She always wanted to see someone do good. In fact, when he called me tripping out on acid screaming, my mother took the phone to try and talk to him. My mother never hated him; she just hated the situation and the end result.

Once I started "dating" again, my mother was aware of the situations I was in. She didn't like it, but she knew, and as she forewarned, once you start having sex, you can't stop. That sordid life eventually caught up with me, and I had to visit the doctor on her dime since I had no insurance. At one point, I had a scare and needed to see someone ASAP. She accompanied me, but not without verbally lashing at me about the kind of life I was living. I cried not only because I was sitting at a doctor's office waiting to find out what the hell was going on, but maybe she was right. In the end, it made good sense to me, after which I started dating my future hubby. But even as I dated him, she tried to dissuade me by trying to tell me to focus solely on school now. Even though I was doing better in school at the time, my mother would always throw in my face that all these kids who were much younger than me had graduated from college while I was still struggling to get a "*vye*"[32] associate degree. I tried to justify it by asking her if she wasn't glad that I had only one man in my life now, and it wasn't physical. She wasn't trying to hear it. One time I was supposed to meet hubby; she put her foot down and refused to let me go. Like I said earlier, she was my child's only source of babysitting, so when she refused to watch her, that was it. So, I had to cancel my plans. He had invited me to a party and even tried to get me to bring my baby girl, but we had just started dating, and I didn't think it was right at the time. Hubby always said that he felt some way about me not showing up and said he was gonna get back at me for that, but then he fell in love with me. I guess marrying me was revenge for the broken date... Lol ☺.

Once hubby and I became serious, he came home and met Ta first. My mother's first impression of him was not really good. She tried to say he looked like a gangsta because he was wearing a motorcycle jacket, and since he didn't stand up straight, she said he was crooked. She said I had hyped him up to her that he was so handsome, and she was not sold on it. It wouldn't be till my graduation party that her sister, Jeannie, and all my cousins were like, what are you talking about? He's a very good-

---

[32] vye-in Haitian Creole means old but, in this sense, means useless or impractical

looking man. She later declined what she said about him and said he looked like the bourgeois in Haiti. Once it was time for graduation, my mother was so very happy that I reached that milestone. Since my mother loved the color red because it symbolized victory, she, Georgie, and I all wore red. During a speech at my graduation party, I singled her out by saying that she always told me, "*Je dois re monter,*" meaning I had to get back up. She was beaming that whole night. Once hubby and I got engaged, my mother was ecstatic. My mother naturally told me that some people said I lacked a chance at finding a husband because I had my baby girl. In fact, a friend said in front of my mother that I was gonna have a hard time finding someone to marry me because I had a child. Well, out of all my friends I was the first to get married. Ta always said, "*tout moun krache nan syèl la epi li tonbe sou pwent nen yo* " meaning everyone spits up in the sky, and it falls right on the tip of their nose. My mother would say, look at GOD. I came back in disgrace and now graduated from college and am getting married. I'll never forget the look on her face as I went to try on my wedding dresses. From her expression, it was evident that this was something she had been waiting for. But before we spent any money, my mother insisted that we conduct a civil ceremony. She said that was the tradition in her family and wanted to make sure the groom would show up before spending beaucoup money. So, we had a civil ceremony performed in my house with my parents, my mother's sister Jeannie, her daughters and their husbands, my uncles, cousin, hubby's mother, aunt, and brother. Ta was truly happy and at peace to plan the wedding of our dreams. Since my parents were paying for most of the wedding requirements, there was no amount spared. The invitations, the venue, the flowers, limousines, our makeup, our hair, my dress, and Georgie's and of course her dress. My dress was a mere $800 at Macy's bridal salon, but that of my mother's was $3000 at a fancy boutique. She didn't want any regular deregular mother of bride two-piece jacket shit. No, my mother wanted something extraordinary, and she got it. A sparkly champagne-colored dress with a matching shawl. I mentioned earlier that hubby, and I had a fight right before the wedding, and I told my mother I was calling it off. I won't even let you imagine her response. She started yelling, "Are you crazy? After the amount of money, we spent??! YOU are getting married."

The day of the wedding finally came, and Ta was in her element as she directed and made sure everything, and everyone was in place. As the limousines entered the circular driveway that she had purposely done just for the occasion, she was pleased. She entered the church with her older sister on the arm of her grandnephew, beaming radiantly. A must in most Haitian weddings was that someone sang *Veni Creator Spiritus,* so she had this bitchy white lady who sang at most Haitian weddings. Madame Blanche, the songstress, was overly domineering regarding what music can and can't be used in church. Without my permission, she switched the music my bridesmaids were supposed to walk to. Yes, I still harbor resentment even though it will be 19 years tomorrow. After the ceremony, we had a grand reception at the then Huntington Townhouse. Whenever we watched my wedding video, which was often, Ta would remark that the reception looked like a "*yon bal trente et un Décembre,"* New Year's Eve party that's how beautiful it was with everyone dancing. The chairs of the reception hall were covered, and a silk ribbon was tied around it. Later, she revealed to me that during the cocktail hour, they informed her that there was a delay getting the coverings for the chairs due to traffic. When they finally made it, she left the cocktail hour and sat in that reception hall and made sure every one of those chairs was covered. Ta didn't dance up a storm because she was so busy making sure everything went well. It was only toward the end of the reception that she kicked off her shoes and danced with one of her best friends. After the wedding festivities the next day, a lot of calls were coming in from various persons raining compliments on my parents (well, Ta since she got the phone) on the wonderful extravagant wedding.

Once all the celebrations were done, we focused on the new baby coming into our lives. When I was around two months pregnant with Cassie, I was told that I might not carry her to term; it was my mother who did a special novena with me (it was in French, and I couldn't read it) every night for the duration of my pregnancy. It was also because of her I purchased and wore a maternity girdle for the seven months of my pregnancy in order to support and keep the fetus in place till delivery. That's why I had to stop wearing it once I reached seven months, so the baby, according to my mother, wouldn't get lazy and stay there. After Cassie's birth, she celebrated the prospect of taking care of a new baby, which she truly enjoyed. She was continuously there for me, particularly as I started to suffer the "baby blues." While watching Cassie, she suggested I step out and get some much-needed air after being cooped up in the house for two weeks after her birth.

Like I wrote before about my father, it was during my hormonal shift that my terrible memories of my "visit to the dentist" reared its ugly head. When I was 10 years old, I had a cavity that had to be taken care of. I think maybe the memories of going there the first time were creeping up, so I knew I didn't want to go. But I knew there was no way I could avoid going there, so I thought to myself if I had just insisted at the office, maybe my mother would take me seriously. Well, when they called me to go in, I started crying, stating that I don't want to go. I don't recall word for word what transpired after that except when my dentist came in the waiting room and physically removed me. My mother, who felt embarrassed, tried to smile it off since I caught the attention of everyone in the waiting room when I started screaming and tried to hold on to the doorway with my sandals flying off my feet as he pulled me off and carried me into his office. He shoved his huge fist down my mouth to the point that I couldn't breathe while yelling at me to stop. Since I had no choice, I just tried to stay calm. Basically, he filled the cavity as I trembled out of fear and blamed me for putting up a fuss for nothing. Since my mother didn't drive at the time, we walked home, and she noticed my lip was busted and bleeding. She said that she would mention it to my father. However, I found out that she told him, and he did nothing. I think I blamed my mother more so than my father because my mother witnessed the abuse. When I mentioned it to her, she turned it around and asked why I was the only one amongst everyone who went there to have this happen. She never liked having bad attention drawn to her. She stated that everyone, including our friends who referred us, went there with no problem except me. I don't care if I was the only one, or if there were hundreds of others, what that man did to me was totally uncalled for. My mother never actually came out to apologize for her part in this mess, but she did acknowledge it. Though I don't condone her actions, I do understand. Here, she was a woman who didn't speak English very well in a foreign country and also abided by and followed her husband, who was the breadwinner and overall decision-maker. She did what she had to and could do.

Ta, as I said earlier, was very much happy that I was married and had a complete family. The only problem was that I stayed married. During our first 10 years, hubby and I went through a lot. One of the major problems in our relationship was that he was not doing his part financially. Like I mentioned in my pop's chapter, that really bothered him, but not my mother to a certain extent. Even though my father worked full time and my mother stayed home, it was something that really bothered her. Particularly, during their usual arguments, papa would throw in her face that she didn't know anything because she was home all day while he was "working his balls" off. Due to this, my mother always insisted that I go to college and be someone that could stand on my own. She wanted me to be independent and self-sufficient. She didn't want me to EVER rely on a man, but because of this, I never really insisted that my husband do his part. I always felt since I work, I too could pay for my own things. I mean, he always paid when we went to the grocery store, but other than that, that was it. He never gave me any money, and I never demanded. So, since he wasn't paying rent to my family and giving me anything, he was scott free enjoying life. It was five years into the marriage when it hit me that I needed to have him pay, well, thanks to my friends. I recall when we discussed it, he said he didn't want to give me money because "I would just spend it on shoes." His aunt, GOD rest her soul, said it didn't matter if I took the money and burned it, stating that I was entitled to it. When I started changing and realizing my "right" my mother did not approve. My take on it was that she didn't want me to see hubby merely as an ATM and rely on him financially. One would expect that she should think differently especially being the wife of a physician. She even said that for someone in her position, she did very well and married a handsome doctor. But she didn't just get with him because of what he could do for her; she loved him as well. I also think Ta didn't want me to rock the boat, probably thinking that I got lucky to find this guy to marry me despite my circumstances. She had the old way of thinking that it was better to just accept this as one of his faults. My mother always used to say that it was because of hubby that she was able to raise her head back in Haitian society. So, in her eyes, I was supposed to tolerate a lot of his bullshit. Like when he went on vacation twice with his fellas without me. After the Vegas trip, he promised he would take me on a vacation, he never did, so I went on my own with my girlfriends. Ta was furious about that; she said a good wife never goes on vacation without her husband. My response to her was that he did it so why shouldn't I. She then blamed hubby and realized a lot of the cracks in my marriage were due to his behavior. Eventually, my mother saw that the marriage didn't look like it was gonna last. I recall her telling me that she doesn't know what she would give for our marriage to be successful.

Since my mother saw that finances were a big issue, she wholeheartedly supported me to return to school. Once I was finished, she looked forward to the new opportunities I had with my additional education. Unfortunately, she was just as disappointed as I was when everything went left. At one point, she came to the mall where I worked as a temporary holiday recruiter, and she saw me approaching people. She said that it broke her heart to see me in such a state. Walking around with "*sapats*[33]" and talking to strangers, trying to get them to apply at Macy's. At one point, I overheard her talking with Georgia when she approached Ta, asking what's wrong with mommy. My mother was like, "Your mother has a bachelor's and a master's that she worked extremely hard for, and she can't find a decent job." How would you feel? My mother tried to remain optimistic, but when this endured a bit longer than a year and hubby got the boot as well, it became extremely hard, and also dealing with her own financial issues didn't help the situation

---

[33] sapats-slippers; house shoes

one bit. By then, my father wasn't able to work the way he did before, so he retired. My mother received an income as well from social security, but it wasn't enough to support their lifestyles which included trying to pay the mortgage on the house. Due to this, they closed and withdrew IRA accounts and took against life insurance policies to survive. As I mentioned in my father's chapter, their mortgage payment had skyrocketed due to some type of financing that went badly. My mother was habitually worried about not being able to pay for their home and even regretted purchasing it. Before they lived in the lap of luxury in Dix Hills, my parents and I had resided in a small ranch home with three bedrooms, one bathroom, and a full basement in Hempstead, Long Island, for 20 years. My mother said she suffered so much embarrassment living there because our home didn't reflect my father's profession. So-called friends of hers would bring people over to make fun of our home. Even my busybody high school bus driver asked why I lived there if my father was a doctor. It got to the point that my mother taught me to lie at school that I stayed with my grandmother during the week in Hempstead and went to see my parents during the weekends. But despite this, my mother truly believed she would one day purchase the home of her dreams, and she did through her effort and papa's money. With a mortgage of almost $10,000, she complained that if she stayed in her little house with a $500 a month mortgage, she would have been able to make it. By the time the house payments started troubling her, she was dealing with something far worse- losing her husband of 40 years.

When my papa passed away, I was the first one to show up in his room. Ta, who was further away at home, showed up 15 minutes later. I can never forget how she busted through the door with much agitation. She never cried though, she just caressed his face and said how beautiful he looked. When I called for a priest, she got angry. She even cursed in creole as he said the final prayer stating that she didn't need to see him. It was the moment we got home that she broke down after speaking to people that were offering their condolences, especially with my daughter, who was away at school. We undertook a lot when preparing to bury papa. I recall watching her as she went to Macy's to purchase his underwear and socks. She looked so small and fragile. Little did I know that I would be at the same Macy's two years later, getting her undergarments to bury her. Ta maintained a calm demeanor until papa's wake, where she fully lost it. She never cried hysterically, but it hit her that he was gone. The days that followed were the real test of how we would get along. Just like I did when I was younger, I slept with her in her room for three months straight. I couldn't leave her alone, especially since I felt responsible for her now. My father's sisters were with us for a while, but then they left, getting back to their own lives, leaving Ta and me. Even though hubby and my youngest were with us, I felt like the grief truly impacted both of us since we were part of the papa bear, mama bear, and baby bear trio. We both tried to lift each other up when we started to falter. The one area I wish I could have provided more support for her was in the aspect of the house. One would think that since papa died, she was set, but all the financial issues they had were left with one insurance policy worth $25,000.00. Enough for two months' worth of mortgage payments, but then what? We went to see a money manager my father had for a particular account that had $150,000.00. He explained to my mother that the balance of the account would not accrue interest large enough to pay the mortgage. Disappointed and baffled, my mother decided to withdraw all the money from the account and close it. Her next stop was social security. As a surviving spouse, she thought that she would get his income added to hers, but to her surprise, she found out that they eliminated her income and replaced it with his. So, she was down to one income. Hell, there were times my mother had to sell some of her beloved jewelry to make ends meet. Even though that hubby and I contributed, it wasn't enough to sustain the household. So, after using the last of the income from my father's account, she made her last mortgage payment in January 2010, after which she decided she would sell her home. Being ole school Haitian, Ta couldn't help but mention that if she had another child, perhaps she would have been a nurse and would have been able to save her from this pain. Those words went through my heart like a knife. I wanted to do any and everything to keep her from this pain. It was around this time that I went full-fledged into focusing and pushing my t-shirt line, thinking that this would blow up and I could save my home for my manman. Even Ta started to believe in me in this aspect. She now encouraged me on something she made fun of in the beginning. One time we were passing a store in the mall, and she said something was missing. I said what, she replied with my t-shirts with a smile. The last year and a half we had together, we grew even closer. We were ready to tackle whatever life had to offer, and we knew we could so long as we had each other.

Early March 2009, she was diagnosed with colon cancer and had an operation to have the damaged tissue removed. While in the hospital, she cried out that she was undergoing too much; she had no money, no husband, and now no health. How much more could she take???!!! She recovered beautifully, and thinking she was okay, we tried to live life day by day and appreciate it even more. Around the spring of 2010, she couldn't walk. At first, we thought it was her arthritis and that she would have to have an operation on her knees. We took her to the ER, and she was admitted for the night. Later after some tests, they found she had thyroid cancer that spread to her spine and brain. This time shit got real. I recall leaving the hospital room with my kids coming back not even 30 seconds later to run into her arms crying. I called all my family and friends and asked them to get down on their knees and pray that GOD wouldn't leave me without my manman. The doctor advised us that she had to be operated on immediately so she would be able to walk again. Thinking she had no other choice and doing what was best, she did the surgery. Unfortunately, the operation took away my manman, and she was never the same. She not only couldn't walk, but couldn't speak coherently, had to be fed, and changed like a baby. The hospital sent her home, but she had to have round-the-clock care, which they didn't supply the first two days. Georgie and I tried to take care of her on our own. Enraged and frustrated, I found myself taking my anger on our dishes. It was around this time that my darling daughter decided to try her hand at shoplifting. Talk about timing; we eventually hired someone fresh from Haiti to watch her from Sunday evening through Friday, as well as an aide hospice provided us with Monday-Friday 9-5 pm. But all the help in the world couldn't stop her from declining even more before our very eyes. It was during this crazy time in my life that I became pregnant. I lost my baby on October 13th, the day my mother was admitted into hospice toward her final journey. Four days later, my mother died. I always felt like my baby's purpose was to provide a piece of me to go with my mother.

Planning this funeral, the responsibility fell solely on me. I didn't have a bank,[34] So thanks to my mother-in-law and family friends, I was able to provide my mother with a lovely and dignified ceremony. Since she always warned me that when she died, she didn't want an open casket wake. I did everything the same day as pops. Instead of a catering hall, I had a small intimate reception at our house.

My mother's death left a void that can never be filled. She was everything to me, my heart, my love, and truly my best friend. Though I have many friends, none have ever come close to my Ta. She was a natural comedian. Everyone who knows me knows about my phobia with pigeons. As I got older, Ta always said that I was scared of the wrong one since pigeon is the Haitian Creole term for a male organ. That bird couldn't do any damage, but the male organ could do a lot. Like, get you "knocked up" or burn you☺☺☺. Despite being ultra bougie,[35]She would always brag that she shared the same name as Jacqueline Bouvier Kennedy; she loved herself some 50cent. She was drawn to him due to his devotion to his grandma, and she also said that he had nice teeth. She genuinely had a good heart and always wanted to see everyone do well. I always gave her credit for not being envious of her friends who were wives of doctors but in better positions financially and socially. If it was me, the green-eyed monster would have made its appearance, but not her, as she never let it bother her. There are some people who said that my mother couldn't live without my father, so she went on to join him, but I know that wasn't the case. Ta wanted to live.

---

[34] bank-lots of money
[35] ultra bougie- extremely high class

Manman was physically and mentally stronger than papa. She went through a lot more that I even forgot to mention that she had open-heart surgery in 2001, and she wanted to be with her family, and it hurts me so much when I think about the suffering she endured mentally and emotionally before the cancer emerged, and then physically. She continually cried out in agony due to the illness that ravaged her body, so much that I reached my breaking point when I turned and prayed to GOD to stop her suffering and take her. But even at the end, she thought of me and gave me her last words of wisdom. "*Pwofite*" meaning to take advantage of life and fully live it.

MY ♥ OF FASHION AND STYLE

Considering that I am the self-proclaimed stiletto queen, I couldn't let my first literary opportunity pass by without mentioning what is a huge part of me ; fashion and style. Ever since I was a little girl, the one thing that always fascinates me is the way a person is dressed. There is a picture I included of me at three years old wearing a striped shirt and plaid pants while my older cousin, Sandra, wore a pink matching pants suit with saddle shoes. I still recall being jealous of her outfit at that young age. One of the first movies I ever saw was *Grease*. Sandy's transformation from good girl gone bad stood out to me. The black skintight spandex pants, black tight off the shoulder top, big hair, and the piece de resistance peep toe red Candies high heels mules. I think that those shoes began my lifelong obsession with high heels. I fell head over heels, no pun intended with those "You better shape up" shoes and wanted a pair so bad. Even though my mother brought me the little girl version, I was glad, but nothing was like the real thing. I vowed that once I grew up, I would wear only those. I was so enthralled by that look on Halloween 1978 that I decided I would be her. But back then, Halloween costumes were limited and consisted of cheap-looking masks and plastic apron types. After my disappointment with Halloween 1977 as Wonder Woman, I refused to ever wear that again. So, I decided I would make up my own. I recall being seven years old with my parents going from store to store trying to find leggings or tight pants to wear but not knowing the exact words to describe it. Now, mind you, this was the late seventies, and as far as I can remember, leggies weren't really a thing then. So, what was a little girl to do other than wear her ballerina leotard and brown dress pants and let out my big dookie braids.

Even after *Grease,* I remained enamored with clothing, particularly girly, sexy fashions. One show that always stood out for me and to this day I watch on YouTube was *Barbara Mandrell and the Mandrell Sisters.* I loved everything about the variety hour show but mostly looked forward to seeing the fashions. One time when I spent the night at my godmother's with her kids, she made us all go to bed at exactly

172

10 pm when the show was on. I recall I was so upset that I started crying because I missed an opportunity to see what they would be wearing. I also had a girl crush on Louise Mandrell, who stood out among her sea of vanilla blonde sisters with her voluptuous figure, dark hair, and sparkly blue eyes. I always wondered why they wouldn't dress her sexier than the younger sister. From what I recall, Barbara was dressed conservative, Louise was semi-conservative, and Irlene wouldn't be conservative at all. Now, as I got older, I realized that they dressed them according to body type. But I wanted to see my favorite in sexier outfits. Around that time, I had gotten the fashion plate for Christmas, and I made up my version of the Mandrell sisters wearing what I wanted. But even as I write this, I recall that the first variety show to peak my interest due to the clothing was *The Sonny and Cher Show*. I must have been three or four years old looking forward to seeing the outrageous and scantily clad Cher. With her long dark hair and lithe body, she made the fashions she wore look effortless. I tried to copy her looks by taking my mother's clothes and heels. Letting my hair out and applying lipstick, I couldn't wait to be a grown-up to wear the fantastic looking fashions.

Along with my love for fashion was my love (to this day still) for food. Most people of Latin American/Caribbean origin view a fat or chubby baby/kid as healthy. My daughter, Georgia, never had a great appetite, so my mother would order special tonics and food to make her gain weight, but all to no avail. But with me, it was never a problem. Weighing in at 8 ½ pounds at birth, I was encouraged to continue eating, and I did. With my father rewarding me with fast food, I ate every bite. Since I was an only child, I never had to worry about sharing as it was all mine. One time at school, we had donuts as a reward, and I took a second one right after eating the first one. My classmate Rena fat-shamed me in front of everyone by telling me to be considerate of those who didn't eat yet. Sharing wasn't part of my vocab. I wasn't grossly overweight, but I was chubby, and it showed. Because I was in Catholic school for most of my youth, I hid behind my uniform. Whenever we had special occasions, then I would scourge around looking for some clothes. Being a girl child plus Haitian, I was always dressed up for any and every occasion. Every Haitian girl can attest to having to wear the dreaded *riban* from birth till mid-teens. Georgia hated wearing ribbons so much so that as a baby, she would pull them out of her hair as my mother watched in bewilderment. Any who, a trip to the doctor would require me to wear a Sunday or party dress and matching ribbons with socks and patent leather shoes. Looking at my kindergarten class pics, I am the only girl wearing a dress with bows in my hair. My mother reveled in dressing me up and treated me like her own living doll. With my daughter, she did the same. They used to call Georgia fashion plate because of the distinct clothing my mother ordered just to send her to kindergarten. So, I can definitely say I got my feminine girly look from her.

As I got older, I wanted to change from the little girl's look and add my spin to it. My mother, GOD bless, didn't know how to dress me since I had my own idea of what I wanted. One time as a freshman in high school, we got to wear regular clothes except for jeans, of course. Jeans in Catholic schools are considered the devil himself. No nuns or priests want to see any kids clad in denim. To them, I guess that wearing jeans is like giving the finger to GOD. Since I didn't have anything, I felt remotely good enough to wear. I asked my mother to pick up something from A & S that I could wear to school when she went shopping. She brought back this ghastly purple, orange, and yellow plaid long accordion skirt, matching sweater vest, and purple blouse. I flipped the FUCK out when I saw that and was so upset that I was resigned to wearing my pink, fluorescent plaid shirt, matching belt, and black dress skirt, fluorescent socks, and flats. Mind you, it was fall/winter of 1985; the fluorescent trend was just dying. But I would rather have been slightly outdated than wear that hideous outfit. From that time, I made sure I picked out my own outfits.

With the eighties came the look of big sweaters/tops and tights for me in the winter. Being that I wore a size 13/14, I knew I couldn't rock any real sexy looks like I wanted to, but that didn't keep me from trying. I would pair my ever-popular Mickey Mouse crop top with shorts and tight white pants even though I had a gut. Once I decided that I wanted to shape up, I chose not to buy any clothes until I reached my goal weight. But even while exercising, I still had to be on point. Once the weight started coming off, I wanted to look like the models in my mother's *Shape* magazine, wearing the low-cut suspender leotard with a t-shirt, tights, and leg warmers. Since I didn't have that exact leotard, I took my bathing suit and wore it backward. Hey! I improvised when it came to being fashionable . Once I felt good about my size, I started buying clothes, but I still dressed like I was still fat. Even though I lost close to 25 lbs., I didn't like what I saw in the mirror. I felt like my hips and thighs were still too big, so I would wear oversize t-shirts with leggings in the spring/summer and wear tank tops with oversized cardigans and jeans underneath in the winter. Since I hated my legs at the time, I wished they were thinner and longer; as a result, I started wearing high heels. Around that time, I was interested in a career in modeling. Being somewhat statuesque and now skinny, I qualified for the job. I recall reading at the time that models always wore heels to elongate their legs, so I adopted that theory quickly. Even though I didn't like the way I looked in pants/jeans, I would wear miniskirts and little cropped tops. My stomach went from a beer belly gut to a sunken trim look with waist definition. My cousin Cricri and I were both battling the bulge at the time; she encouraged me to flaunt my abs by stating I had achieved the unattainable flat stomach. Prince's "U Got the Look" video had just come out, and I was mesmerized by Sheila E's look. Her all-white ensemble of a tight, sleeveless, mock turtleneck half skirt with one-legged leggings. I immediately took scissors to my pink tank top and started wearing it daily. Every day when I came home from school, I wore that top and my acid wash skirt mini skirt. I even wore it out once or twice. It was the one outfit I felt sexy in despite being close to skin and bones. At 5'7.5 and 115lbs, I was perfect for modeling but not so good for an everyday look. Once I started eating normally, I gained a healthier weight of 125lbs. The one bad result of the extreme dieting was that it left me with a very small chest. Before I dieted, I was probably a big B small C, but since I'm pear-shaped, they really didn't stick out. Once I lost the weight, I lost a good portion of the tities as well. I didn't really think it made a difference since I had a little something, and I wasn't completely flat. But my cousins, who were busty, would tease me as well as a friend and classmate, Lidia Antonao. She was in awe of her own big boobies strutting around with her chest sticking out; she would tease me mercilessly. Since my initials are S.T., she would say that stood for small tits 😊.   My friend and shopping buddy, Anna, had a real hourglass figure. Next to her, I looked like a little boy. One time, we went shopping, and I tried a cute mini skirt combo with a matching top in a small size. The skirt fit perfectly, but I was engulfed in the top despite being a small size. I quickly became obsessed with boobs and started wearing a full padded bra under my tops to provide a more even look to my figure.

One of the reasons my friendship with Anna worked so well was our love of "slutty dressing." A term we coined ourselves. Kelly Bundy from *Married With Children* was our muse. We didn't want to hide our bodies behind our clothes. We wanted to show them off. What I'm about to say now is gonna be harsh, but it's my truth. Before I reveal it, I want it to be known that I never ever shared this with my two daughters, especially Georgia. As a little girl, after watching an episode of *Charlie's Angels* when they went undercover as hookers, I wanted to be one too due to the clothes. The outfits were just my kind of style; overly sexy and skintight. Plus, the makeup was not understated but flashy. I knew I would dress that way when I grew up. When I was 17, I was stuck at home trying on clothes. I wore my black mini skirt and white crop top with my white high heel boots over the knee that laced up in the back like Prince's proteges wore . Disgustedly, my father told my mother that I looked like a hooker. A small part of me felt that I had accomplished my childhood goal. But even after losing weight, I didn't dress that way in public because, being young and wanting to fit in; I dressed like my peers around me. I did the preppy thing for about a minute. It wasn't until Anna came into the picture that I felt free to dress the way I wanted. Having Anna as my co-conspirator gave me the courage to be who I really was. But I must say that Anna was the real fashion maven when it came to putting outfits together. In essence, I really bit[36] off her style. Where I would just put a basic skirt and top, Anna would add the flair. Since we were so much into fashion, we would trade and share our clothing with each other. I once loaned her my black mini and cropped black zipper top that I never wore. The next time I saw it, she had on a sleeveless red short catsuit with a black zipper on the front, the black mini skirt over it, red flats, and used the zipper top as a jacket. Stunned, I mentally decided I would wear that outfit ASAP. Because of her, I started wearing jeans to the knee. We brought jeans, cut them off at the legs, and rolled them up. Just like the character Baby in *Dirty Dancing*, Anna was obsessed with that movie. She also got the daisy duke shorts from that as well as the Keds sneakers and the slip on. I think she came up with the footless tights on her own. She paired those tights with just about anything from miniskirts to the jeans to the knee.

At the time, *Rags to Riches*, a musical comedy about a multimillionaire businessman adopting five orphan girls, had just stopped playing on TV, but I still had my copies of the show on VHS. Anna and I both loved the show and were drawn to the outfits of the sexy bombshell daughter Diane. She always paired her dresses or skirts with colored coordinated capri tights. Plus, when she would accessorize, she did it perfectly, very matchy. One outfit she wore on a date was red spandex pants, a matching floral crop tight top, and black high heels. We both vowed before the end of the year that we would get those spandex pants. If I remember correctly, I did purchase them and attempted to wear them under my uniform. My uniform had a bit of red in it, but knowing the dress code and the punishment for violating it, I decided not to go that route. As I mentioned about school, I think every high school has a contrast of patterns, shapes, or colors teams versus each other. One year, my team took on the persona of the city, so I decided I would dress as the hip and trendy "Greenwich villager." I wore my black and white Italian boy mini skater skirt. I know right, A black girl wearing Italian boy. SMH. Black spandex shorts underneath, black tight off the shoulder tops (we were obsessed with those), my black zipper top as a jacket with some slouchy socks, and my booties. The Dean of Students, Sr. Kathryn was

---

[36] bit-copied

commenting on everyone's outfits, and when she saw me, she said out loud, 'I know what you are.' Hint hint. If I had been woke[37] back then, I would have called her out for racial defamation. Because I'm Black, I have to be a hooker???? I know me being mad over something that totally contradicts my plans and thought of slutting dressing, but there was no need to call me out in front of everyone, especially since I was one of the only Black students there.

Whenever Anna and I made plans to go out, the first and foremost thing we would do is plan our outfits. Every outfit had a certain look with hair and make-up. If we wore pink, we'd wear pink lipstick, red of course red lipstick, and yellow would be gold lipstick. Certain outfits required a ponytail, a half-ponytail, or full out hair. Both of us were only children and had somewhat strict parents, so since we both were desperate for a social life that included guys, we came up with a "brilliant" plan of getting dressed up and walking around the local mall. We thought that would increase our chances of finding someone. Anna wore an all-red pants outfit. A tight surplice top that emphasized her boobs and loose pants with a hat and heels. That's another thing she taught me… that if you wear a tight top, the bottom should be somewhat loose. I wore a red cinched waist jacket with a black leather mini, midnight black sheer pantyhose, and red high heels. Talk about tacky red heels and black pantyhose. SMH. Fortunately, we didn't meet anyone, just a lot of cattle calls.

By the summer of 1989, Anna & I were no longer friends. Two spoiled only children can be a lethal combination, so I forged on alone in my fashion choices adopting many of the styles and trends I learned from her. The only problem is that I really stood out among my friends who didn't reflect my slutty dressing, and due to this, I would garner a lot of attention from the guys. One time we went to our local community college to see about registering one of my friends for the fall. I was wearing daisy dukes denim shorts, a sky blue top with a string that's tied at the shoulders with no bra, so my then perky bosoms stood out with

---

[37] woke-awake about racism

keds. Again it was summer, so there was absolutely no one on campus. We decided to look around a bit as we were leaving. Why did we have to run into the football team that was just finishing practice? Oh, Lordt! A group of maybe 40 young men, mostly Black, and all with something to say about/to me. Though I usually loved being the center of attention, this was a bit much. I was kinda mortified. If I was white or a bit lighter, my face would have turned red. My one friend Monique was laughing hysterically, while my other friend, Sheree, stood by silently. I would find out from Monique, Sheree would question why the guys would always focus on me and not on them. That's one thing I have got to give to Monique; even though we aren't speaking now (long story), she never was the jealous type. She would enjoy the attention I got, plus we were never into the same guys, to begin with. Another result of my slutting dressing was it had guys thinking I was something more than I was. One time at the college union, us girls and guys were sitting around and discussing sex. When the topic of virginity came up, most of the guys were shocked that I was still a virgin despite my appearance. They were dumbfounded when conservatively (well, more conservative than me), Monique and Sheree both admitted they weren't virgins. Never ever judge a book by its cover.

With all this talk about hoeish dressing, you're probably wondering how I went from that to being a covered up kimar[38] wearing sista. Well, it was definitely a process. Even though Hakeem was attracted to me because of the way I looked once we became serious, he encouraged me to start dressing like the Islamic sisters. It was due to his influence that I broke the then tradition of wearing white before summer. He would say it was the color of angelic beings and that it should be worn whenever. Right before the big party where I lost my virginity, I went to Contempo Casuals and purchased a mid-length gypsy white skirt and matching top. But in true Sybil fashion, it had a tight knot emphasizing the waist and hips. When he saw it, he was proud, and all his friends were in awe that he got me to wear all white. He then started saying that I would look nice in the baggy jeans like all the little hood girls in the

---

[38] kimar-the formal garb Muslim women wear

neighborhood wore, so I started shopping at foreign places like Aeropostale and The Gap. Under his careful manipulation and being an overly eager girlfriend trying to impress her boyfriend, I went from rocking booty shorts to dressing like one of the guys. I still remember when I purchased my first pair of sneakers at Nike or Footlocker, I was with Nakeisha, who already dressed like that, so I used her as guidance. When it came time to purchase, there was the choice of black Reeboks or Balloons. I didn't know the difference except that the price of the Reebok was higher than the Balloons. When I chose the Balloons, Nakeisha's eyes bulged out, telling me hell no. The Reeboks were the choice to make. I think that's part of the charm of hood culture, dressing in expensive shit despite your financial circumstances. Summertime, I rocked the white gypsy outfit, but since the original top showed off my stomach to my boyfriend's relief, I replaced it with t-shirts. I started wearing my mother's empire dresses adding footless tights here and there. Once my clothing changed, Hakeem started in on my hair. I had 100% super processed hair which, of course, didn't mesh with his Asiatic Black man philosophy, so since he mentioned the natural waves looked nice, I tried it and adopted it from time to time. As far as makeup was concerned, it was no longer an issue since I no longer used it.

With the dedication to the deen increasing, I went from hood to ultra-conservative. I started wearing long skirts, boots, and head wraps. Since my hair was considered a thing of beauty only my mate could see, I had to cover it up. SMH. Once word got out that I was a full-blown Muslim, friends called me asking if they could have my clothes. One thing I had to admit was that I had quite a collection of clothes. Some I kept and would wear around Hakeem, but most I did end up giving away. When we moved into the "community," we were allowed to continue to wear our regular clothing in the apartment, but when we went out, we had to wear the kimar. That eventually changed as well. One thing that should have stood out but didn't was the cult's continuous change of image. From what I recall, they adopted the ideals of long ago in biblical times. They used biblical verses to confirm everything. Then suddenly, we went from the kimar to dressing like Indians. The women would wear long Indian tunic tops with matching pants (could not be short or tight, of course) with a sheer veil. We were also allowed to wear all types of colors instead of sticking to white, brown, black, and beige like before. The men could continue dressing as they did, but they would add Native American accessories to them like cowboy boots and suede jackets with fringes. Then we were no longer Ansaaru Allah Community but Nuwaubians Nations. But the real cherry on the sundae was when we had to go to a celebration that the "Lamb" was having at his estate. From what I recall, it was his birthday, and in my opinion, if you are the so-called divine leader of your people, don't you think you would provide food and beverage for them instead of charging for it. I mean, when Jesus had a multitude of people come to hear him speak, HE didn't say that everybody should give five cents, and I will produce the food. No! HE took the five loaves and two fishes and made more than enough for everyone without requesting any payment. Not saying this "Lamb" should have; I mean, COULD have performed this miracle, but he sure as hell didn't have to charge us for food and drink. Sorry, I know that was a long rant, but I had to go there. Anyway, the "Lamb" specified that the women had to wear high heels. I remember protesting wearing heels since Hakeem was shorter than I, but I was told I had to. When I look back at it now, to me, he wanted to get a better look at his female followers so that he could pick out those he would have his way with.

By the time I left and went home, I was in a state of limbo when it came to my clothing. Being pregnant, I couldn't exactly rock sexy clothing. I wore some of my mother's empire waist dresses until she took me maternity shopping. Since it was summer, she got me two short sets, pregnancy pants, and a long white romper. Once fall set in, I felt more comfortable dressing in baggy clothes because I was pregnant. So, I purchased a man's set of denim overalls. I would wear them regularly with a top underneath to show off my stomach, or if I really wanted to dress hood, I would wear my long shirt and walla! It looked like I was wearing baggy jeans and a top. As I anxiously waited for my baby's birth, I watched TV to see what was in style at the time. I looked forward to being able to wear stylish outfits once I gave birth. The only problem with that was the weight that I gained. I'm not one of these females who drop the pregnancy weight quickly once the baby is born. (Thank goodness TLC had come out then, so I was able to mask my weight wearing huge baggy pants with colorful tees, socks, and suspenders.) No, I'm always left carrying the brunt of the weight, so in order to get back to what I knew, I looked like I joined Lucille Roberts and came up with my own diet. Within six months of her birth, I lost most of the pregnancy weight. Once I did, I was back in the business of being fashionable and stylish. But with time, age, and I guess motherhood, the slutting dressing went out the window. Well, sort of. I mean, this was the time of going to clubs for me, so slutting dressing now had its place. I must say I had more than my share of little black dresses and poom poom shorts[39] to wear to the club. Despite being a mother, I continued to stay on point when it came to my fashion choices. When I met hubby, I was dressed quite conservatively for the pool party/barbecue. Everyone was dressed in bikinis and bathing suits while I showed up in denim daisy dukes (that's right, I got them back☺), a tight shirt that said Mon Cherie, and socks and sneakers. It's so ironic that I wore that shirt because when we became serious and to this day, our pet names for each other are *"Cherie."* This time in my/our relationship, I refused to allow any of his input on my attire to ever influence me. Even now, after 19 years of marriage, he will try and say something, but I don't really pay him any mind. Like I recently purchased a red dress for my birthday, and he remarked, how many red dresses do you need? Red is my favorite color, and I try to wear a new red dress for every birthday. Needless to say, I have quite a few. Now that we're getting older, his remarks towards my clothing are "that's really not age appropriate," but I just brush it off. But even before him mentioning age, I now take that into consideration. Now that I'm getting up there, there are a lot of things that I won't wear and things I never thought I would wear.

Shoes, the staple and love of most women, wouldn't really influence my life till the mid-90s to early 2000s. I blame it on *Sex and the City,* which I think most women would agree. Before then, I usually wore flats or

---

[39] poom poom-extremely short shorts

sandals, reserving the heels for special occasions such as parties, weddings, etc. The only other place I wore high heels was for work. I just remembered when I first started job hunting at 18; I wore a red suit which consisted of a cropped jacket matching somewhat tight pants, and a tight black sweetheart top with big hair and red lipstick. Wearing black satin pumps with rhinestones on the front. GOD, I think if I saw someone come in dressed like that for an interview, I would ask three or four times if they were applying for the right job. But most of my shoes at the time were for formal socializing instead of every day. Plus, being that most of the guys I liked were usually my height or shorter, I didn't really focus on purchasing heels. Well, one time, I did purchase a pair of white super high heel booties. I couldn't wait to pair them with my mint green jeans and top till I tried them on and realized that I was way too tall. The heels must have been five inches, and then some. Now, what I have to say goes for me and me only, but I will not wear heels higher than four inches and some change. When I wear five inches or more, I feel massive and awkward. I know coming from the self-proclaimed stiletto queen, this sounds off, but it works for me. There actually was a time that I tried to find heels that were two inches and none higher because I felt funny being taller than hubby. My mother, who was 5'6', would always rub in my face that my father at 6'2 was the perfect height for her and her high heels, but I had a "short man." Finally, it hit me that I was gonna be me, and I wouldn't let his height interfere with my shoes. When I started working full time, most of my pay would go towards what I had on my feet, and I made no qualms about reserving them for special occasions. I wore them every day, and being that I'm semi-tall, I really stood out. I recall one place I once worked; this girl asked me why I always wore heels to work every day. When Long Island women come to work, they really don't put any effort, I've noticed, regardless of the pay scale. They usually adopt the "uniform" of khakis and clogs /sandals in the summer or winter khakis and booties. When that girl asked me, I replied, "I'm a lady, what do you expect?" When my father was in the hospital that terrible summer of 2008, I didn't skimp nor spare on my appearance. In fact, I did it even more because I had a group of admirers working in the hospital. I wore all types of heels and then some. Even my friends that came to the hospital will vouch that I continued slaying despite the circumstances I was in. My mother would say that this was a distraction for me during that difficult time. It was my mother who taught me from a young age to always be overdressed than under. Even at my father's funeral, my friend remarked that my mother, with her dress and hat, looked like a character from *Dynasty*. Very elegant and chic. Even regarding death, my mother didn't take her appearance lightly. As I mentioned appearance, whereas I will go out, however, my mother wouldn't. I know this is a very bad habit, but if I have somewhere I'm going later or if it's that time of the month, I usually look pretty disheveled and not put together. One time while I was dating hubby, we had plans later that evening, so I went out with my mother and daughter. I wore baggy sweats, a hoodie, my hair was wrapped up with a stocking cap and hat over it, walking on the backs of my over five years old Reebok pump sneakers. My mother walked behind me and watched me in horror. She said next time I go out with her, either I dress better or stay in the car. In my mind, I tend to save my pretty look for my special events, and such which really isn't good because it's usually at your worst that you run into an ex, and I have.

As far as shoes are concerned, for me, they are more than what you wear on your feet. To me, they are as much of an expression of yourself as your clothes and hair. For me, high heels/stilettos represent confidence, femininity, and power. I know that's why I chose them to represent my company BaBombshell. For me being a confident, strong, and sexy female is a power all in itself. But now, as with anything, I welcome variety. There was a time that I would only wear high heels; slingbacks, ankle straps, d'orsay, mules with or without peep toes, wedges, pumps, booties, and full boots all had to be heels. Now at this stage of the game, I like and welcome an assortment. At one point, I said I would never wear uggs, but I wear them now as well as sandals and flip-flops. When it came to the flip-flops, I was totally turned off. I recall seeing drug addicts wearing them back in the day, or you would save them for the beach. Now they are very fashionable, particularly with special designs or touches added on. I usually reserve wearing them with my maxi dresses. Yep, miss shows everything off now wears maxi dresses which are very flattering to a tall and somewhat shapely (don't forget lack of tities) female like me. I now realize that I can look good without showing everything off. However, I still like to be sexy (I don't think that will ever change), but now it's about being classy. I now realize that there is something so sexy about a woman who carries herself well. Slutty and trampish have been replaced with sophisticated and chic. It's exactly how I want my t-shirt/clothing line to be thought of as well. Maybe it's time, maybe it's experience, and maybe it's a little of both as my mother would always say that with every age, your way of thinking changes. Now before I wrap this up, I just want to add my list of likes and dislikes when it comes to style.

LIKES & DISLIKES

1. Ruffles are a small bosom girl's best friend underwire without padding is not.

2. If you're gonna show cleavage and leg, don't do both at the same time because it looks overly trampy. When I mention this, I mean wearing a short skirt with your tities hanging out. Choose one or the other.

3. Learn how to recycle. Since I'm not a celeb, I have the luxury of wearing things more than once. When it comes to special occasions, I look at one of my many social circles and see if I've worn it before; if not, then I can wear it again.

4. Speaking of recycling, don't throw anything out because it's no longer in style, throw it out because you hate it. I have a beige and white striped dress that I got in 1994 when they were the rage that I still rock in the summer. Also, have a skort/romper my mother brought me after Georgia was born that I still wear when on vacation and get many compliments on. Again, I love most of my clothes, so I'll continue to wear them.

5. You don't have to splurge to look good. I honestly purchase a lot of my clothing online or via catalog, and they're not that pricey. One place I shop from, VENUS has a lot of nice outfits for not so high prices. As well as boohoo.com. It's how YOU make the outfit look. You can either cheapen an expensive outfit or add value to a cheap outfit.

6. Speaking of labels wearing too much of a particular label or even a variety doesn't look that good. I know labels to some people represent everything but take it one at a time.

7. Peep-toe mules look sexiest with midi skirts, summer dresses, pencil skirts, pedal pushers, gauchos, wide legs, and of course the straight leg and skintight. But not pairing with miniskirts looks really trampy.

8. Tattoos. Where do I begin? Let me say I admire and respect that line of work. As someone who is semi creative, I truly see it as a work of art. But not for me, I hate excessive tattoos especially on women. For Black folks, it's ghetto, and for Whites, it looks trashy. Men can get away with it because they have the option of covering it up. e.g., a tuxedo, suit, or shirt and pants. However, women with dresses short or long, slit or not, backless, cleavage showing you can't hide them.

9. Don't like white flip-flops because they get too dirty and look trashy.

10. Don't like red sneakers at all looks very ghetto.

11. I HATE gladiator's sandals that go all the way up the leg. Whether high heeled or flat looks, very tacky as well as high heel thong sandals. I hate them.

12. With Kim Kardashian's ass as the second coming, I too jumped on the big ass bandwagon and tried to make my already large posterior bigger with painful butt lifted panties. (Hubby said I looked like I was gonna pass out when I wore it) Till I realized

that an exaggerated ass is vulgar and obscene. Now don't get me wrong, if you have a natural big ass like my cousin Yanik who wears like two girdles to reduce the size, more power to you, and be proud. But if you're going out of your way to get surgery and wear the push ass panties, please stop.